FOURTH GRADE MATH

Table of Contents

Introduction

Mathematics skills are utilized in every aspect of an individual's life, whether a student or an adult. These skills, however, involve more than just the computation of numbers. Organization, investigation, logical reasoning, and communication are also basic skills associated with mathematics. Students must develop a solid foundation in basic mathematics skills in order to meet the challenges of learning. Once armed with these tools, they can face new situations with confidence in their ability to solve problems and to make decisions.

The *Fourth Grade Math* program is offered to develop and strengthen mathematics skills. Each page provides practice in one specified skill. The worksheet can be used to assess students' understanding of the concept before or after the classroom lesson, or it can be used by students who might benefit from additional practice, either at home or school.

Organization

Nine units cover the basic mathematics skills taught in the fourth grade. Students begin with a review of place value and the skills needed to add and subtract numbers. They move on to practice skills dealing with multiplication and division. Students them proceed to exploring elements of time and graphs. Finally, the book focuses on measurement, geometry, fractions, and decimals. Fun, thematic worksheet titles attract students' interest. One page at the end of each unit is devoted solely to word problems which show how the learned skill might be applied to a real-world situation. These problems also provide practice in using a variety of problem-solving strategies.

Special Features

Each worksheet serves as practice for only one basic mathematics skill. Students who may need additional practice could benefit from these pages. Each page in the *Fourth Grade Math* book also ends with a word problem. These problems deal only with the skill students are practicing. These word problems also provide examples of how mathematics skills can be applied to the real world.

Use

This book is designed for independent use by students who have had instruction in the specific skills covered in the lessons. Copies of the worksheets can be given to individuals, pairs of students, or small groups for completion. The worksheets can also be given as homework for reviewing and reinforcing basic mathematics skills.

To begin, determine the implementation that fits your students' needs and your classroom structure. The following plan suggests a format for use:

1. Explain the purpose of the worksheets to your class.
2. Review the mechanics of how you want students to work with the exercises.
3. Review the specific skill for the students who may not remember the process for successful completion of the computation.
4. Introduce students to the process and to the purpose of the activities.
5. Do a practice activity together.
6. Discuss how students can use the skill as they work and play.

Additional Notes

1. A letter to parents is included on page 4. Send it home with the students and encourage them to share it with their parents.
2. Have fun with the pages. Math should be an enjoyable adventure that helps students grow, not only in math, but in their confidence and their ability to face new and challenging experiences.

Dear Parent,

Mathematics skills are important tools that your child will use throughout his or her life. These skills encompass more than just the computation of numbers. They involve the ability of individuals to organize, investigate, reason, and communicate. Thus, your child must develop a strong foundation of basic mathematics skills in the elementary grades so that he or she can expand and build on these skills to help navigate through the life experiences.

During the year, your child will be learning and practicing many mathematics skills in class. Some of the skills include adding and subtracting numbers with three or more digits, multiplying, dividing, adding and subtracting fractions and decimals, and working with standard and metric units of measurement. After exploring the concepts associated with these basic skills, your child will bring home worksheets, whether completed in class or to be completed at home, designed to further practice these skills. To help your child progress at a faster rate, please consider the following suggestions:

- Together, review the work your child brings home or completes at home. Discuss any errors and encourage your child to correct them.
- Encourage your child to make up word problems which apply to newly learned skills.
- Guide your child to see why it is important to learn math by pointing out ways that math is used in everyday life.
- Play games and solve puzzles with your child that utilize math skills.

Thank you for your help. Your child and I appreciate your assistance and reinforcement in this learning process.

Cordially,

Name _____ Date _____

Solve.

1. 16
      $+\ 8$

2.   6
         $\times\ 9$

3. $5\overline{)25}$

4. 7.28
       $-\ .33$

5. 1,000
      $\times\quad 4$

6. $2\overline{)54}$

7.   67
         $\times\ 3$

8. $\frac{5}{8}$
       $+\frac{1}{8}$

9. 197
      $\times\ 29$

10. 1,364
         528
       $+\ 180$

11. 18,247
       $-\ 4,986$

12. $2.45
        $+\ 9.32$

13. 1,786
        $\times\quad 4$

14. $5\overline{)419}$

15. $3\frac{2}{7}$
        $+1\frac{3}{7}$

16. 34.03
        $+\ 6.89$

17. 372
       $\times\ 21$

18. $6\frac{7}{9}$
        $-4\frac{4}{9}$

19. $8 \times 0 =$ _____

20. $135 + 27 =$ _____

21. $25 \div 6 =$ _____

22. $544 \div 8 =$ _____

23. $8,549 - 7,234 =$ _____

24. $84 \times 7 =$ _____

25. $3 + (5 + 4) =$ _____

26. $\frac{6}{10} - \frac{3}{10} =$ _____

••••• WORKING ON PROBLEM SOLVING •••••

✎ Choose the strategy and solve.

1. In one month, Karin spends $50 on gas for her car, $22 for parking, and $48 on bus tickets. About how much money does Karin spend on transportation in a month?

_____

2. Bianca watered the lawn of one house for $\frac{1}{3}$ hour and $\frac{2}{3}$ hour at a second house. What fraction of an hour did Bianca spend watering the lawn? How many minutes is this?

_____

3. Elena rides 38 kilometers to work each day. How many kilometers is this in a five-day work week?

_____

4. At Koyoko's workplace, there are 144 workers. If there are 8 workers in each office, how many offices are there?

_____

5. Sally works as a caterer. Her punch bowl holds 6 quarts of liquid. She buys 2 pints of juice, 2 quarts of ginger ale, and 1 gallon of sherbet for a punch. Will all of the ingredients fit into the bowl?

_____

6. Maria needs a total of 4 eggs in her muffin batter. She has already added 3 eggs. What fraction of eggs has she already added to the batter?

_____

7. Joseph bought some office supplies. He paid $3.98 for paper, $1.79 for staples, and $1.59 for paper clips. How much change did he get from a ten-dollar bill?

_____

8. Edgar begins work at 8:15 A.M. He eats his lunch from 12:15 P.M. until 12:45 P.M. and then goes back to work. He quits working for the day at 4:30 P.M. How long does Edgar work each day?

_____

·········· DIVE INTO NUMBERS ···········

 Complete to name each number.

1.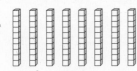

____ hundreds ____ ones

_____

2.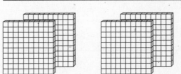

____ tens ____ ones

_____

3.

____ tens ____ ones

_____

4.

____ hundreds ____ ones

_____

 Complete.

5. 60 = ___ ones   **6.** 400 = ___ tens   **7.** 900 = ___ hundreds

8. 800 = ___ tens   **9.** 7,000 = ___ hundreds   **10.** 3,200 = ___ tens

Write the value of each number in four ways.

11. 3,800   **12.** 1,400   **13.** 4,500

_____   _____   _____

_____   _____   _____

_____   _____   _____

_____   _____   _____

Real World Connection

Solve.

14. The park workers add 37 hundred gallons of water to the pool. Write in standard form the number of gallons of water workers add to the pool.

_____

Name _____ Date _____

• • • • • • • • • • • • • • • IN THE CITY • • • • • • • • • • • • • •

Express each number in two other ways.

1. 10,000 + 600 + 7

_____

_____

2. ninety thousand, five hundred

_____

_____

3. 34,069

_____

_____

4. 300,000 + 7,000 + 800 + 60 + 4

_____

_____

5. four hundred thousand,
six hundred seventy-three

_____

_____

6. 20,483

_____

_____

Write the value of the digit 4 in each number in two ways.

7. 3,456

_____

_____

8. 48,062

_____

_____

9. 59,241

_____

_____

Write the value of the underlined digit in two ways.

10. 4<u>3</u>7,215

_____

_____

11. 96,3<u>0</u>7

_____

_____

12. 4<u>8</u>,162

_____

_____

Real World Connection

Solve.

13. Two hundred eighty-nine thousand, three hundred
people live in the city of Newton. Write the number
in standard form and in expanded form.

_____

Name _____   Date _____

 Name the period shown by the underlined digits.

1. 1,<u>667</u>,495   **2.** <u>657</u>,604,980   **3.** 258,418,<u>732</u>

_____   _____   _____

Write the number that is 1,000,000 more.

4. 67,016,018 _____   **5.** 639,540,086 _____

6. 20,876,905 _____   **7.** 899,632,400 _____

Write the number that is 10,000,000 less.

8. 23,579,410 _____   **9.** 845,270,100 _____

10. 47,850,298 _____   **11.** 987,506,460 _____

Study the number in the box. Write _true_ or _false_.

| 18 million, 6 hundred |

12. The standard form is 18,600.   _____

13. The expanded form is 10,000,000 + 8,000,000 + 600.   _____

14. The digit in the thousands place is 6.   _____

15. The value of the digit in the hundred-thousands place is 0.   _____

Real World Connection

Solve.

16. In a science book, Clark read that the star Alpha Herculis is estimated to be six hundred ninety million miles in diameter. What number did Clark write?

_____

•••••••••••••••• GET IN ORDER ••••••••••••••••

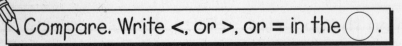

Compare. Write <, or >, or = in the ◯.

JUDGE ORTIZ

1. 2,541 ◯ 986   **2.** 274 ◯ 279

3. 8,642 ◯ 764   **4.** 2,329 ◯ 3,329

5. 62,911 ◯ 58,012   **6.** 8,116 ◯ 18,611

Write the numbers using the symbol that means *is less than*.

7. 52; 56   **8.** 76; 67   **9.** 1,339; 1,239

_____   _____   _____

Write the numbers using the symbol that means *is greater than*.

10. 84; 48   **11.** 2,049; 2,094   **12.** 26,784; 26,847

_____   _____   _____

Write each group of numbers in order from least to greatest.

13. 785; 763; 812   **14.** 175; 136; 149   **15.** 959; 990; 995; 929

_____   _____   _____

16. 4,618; 4,390; 4,364   **17.** 17,642; 17,640; 17,697; 17,604

_____   _____

Real World Connection

Solve.

18. The size of Acadia National Park in Maine is 41,409 acres. The size of Mesa Verde National Park in Colorado is 52,085 acres. Which park is larger?

_____

Name _____ Date _____

•••••••••• NUMBER ROUNDUP ••••••••••

Estimate by rounding to the nearest ten or to the nearest ten cents.

1. 52 _____   **2.** $3.78 _____   **3.** 66 _____

4. $1.45 _____   **5.** 87 _____   **6.** $1.34 _____

7. 555 _____   **8.** 226 _____   **9.** 905 _____

Estimate by rounding to the nearest hundred or to the nearest dollar.

10. 457 _____   **11.** 242 _____   **12.** $8.46 _____

13. 233 _____   **14.** $3.05 _____   **15.** 869 _____

Estimate by rounding to the nearest thousand.

16. 6,816 _____   **17.** 2,310 _____   **18.** 2,737 _____

19. 1,421 _____   **20.** 3,500 _____   **21.** 7,984 _____

Real World Connection

Solve.

22. The ranch hands at K Bar Z have to gather about 380 cattle. What is the least number and the greatest number of cattle the ranch hands could gather?

_____

··FOLLOW THE RIVER TO PROBLEM SOLVING··

Choose the strategy and solve.

1. The longest river in China is the Yangtze River. It is three thousand, nine hundred fifteen miles long. Write the number in standard form.

_____

2. Paul has kayaked over 23,572 meters in a weekend race. Write the number of meters in expanded form.

_____

3. The Mississippi River is 2,348 miles long. The Missouri River is 2,315 miles. Write the number sentence using the *greater than* symbol to show which river is longer.

_____

4. Joel's hiking club walked along a river 1,024 meters today. On the day before, they walked 100 meters less than this. Write the number of meters they walked yesterday.

_____

5. The world's longest river is the Nile. It is about 4,160 miles long. Estimate the length to the nearest hundred miles.

_____

Name _____ Date _____

• • • • • • • • • • • • COMPUTE THE FACTS • • • • • • • • • • • •

Follow the rule. Complete.

1.

Add 5	
Input	Output
1	6
3	
5	
6	

2.

Subtract 3	
Input	Output
9	
7	
5	
3	

3.

Subtract 9	
Input	Output
12	
15	
16	
18	

4.

Add 8	
Input	Output
9	
8	
7	
3	

5.

Add 2	
Input	Output
4	
5	
6	
7	

Find the sum or difference.

6.   0
    + 5

7.   2
    + 9

8. 14
    − 7

9.   8
    + 5

10. 16
    − 8

11. 13
    − 7

Real World Connection

Write the number sentence and solve.

12. Mr. Alholm has 7 computers in his classroom.
He gets 8 more computers. How many computers
does Mr. Alholm have in his classroom now?

_____

Addition and Subtraction: Facts Review

Math 4, SV 8048-0

Name _____   Date _____

• • • • • • • • • • "SUM" BOOK MATH • • • • • • • • • • •

Find the sum. Check by grouping the addends differently.

1. 3 + (5 + 4) = ☐

2. (2 + 7) + 8 = ☐

3. 4 + (1 + 8) = ☐

4. (4 + 5) + 6 = ☐

5. 9 + (2 + 7) = ☐

6. (7 + 3) + 4 = ☐

Look for tens. Find the sum.

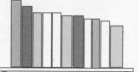

7. 3
    2
  + 7

8. 2
    8
  + 6

9. 5
    5
  + 6

10. 9
    1
  + 7

11. 7
    3
  + 4

12. 6
    4
  + 3

13. 2
    8
  + 4

14. 7
    6
  + 3

15. 4
    6
  + 8

16. 3
    2
  + 8

17. 3
    5
  + 8

18. 7
    2
  + 7

19. 4
    1
  + 6

20. 8
    1
  + 9

21. 2
    6
  + 5

Real World Connection

Write the number sentence and solve.

22. Kevin keeps a reading log of books he reads. In September he reads 4 books. In October he reads 3 books. In November he reads 5 books. How many books does Kevin read altogether?

_____

Name _____ Date _____

·········· IT'S ABOUT THE NEWS ··········

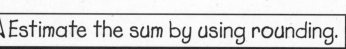
Estimate the sum by using front-end digits.

1. $5.23 + $2.78 = _____   **2.** 418 + 310 = _____

3. $7.03 + $1.64 = _____   **4.** 579 + 208 = _____

Estimate the sum by using rounding.

5. $7.25 + $0.98 = _____   **6.** 362 + 194 = _____

7. 615 + 374 = _____   **8.** 2,356 + 4,600 = _____

Estimate the sum by rounding.

9. $9.23   **10.**   627   **11.** $8.04   **12.**   764
       + 1.85   + 312   + 3.69   + 149

13.   2,515   **14.** $12.78   **15.**   1,506   **16.**   3,234
       + 4,867   + 13.02   + 2,368   + 1,723

Real World Connection

Write the number sentence and solve.

17. Janice delivers 55 newspapers on Saturday and
86 newspapers on Sunday. About how many
newspapers does she deliver each weekend?

_____

Name _____ Date _____

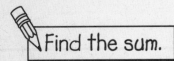 ·········· **THE ADDITION RACE** ············

Find the sum.

1. 46 + 13	**2.** 16 + 65	**3.** 27 + 38	**4.** 67 + 29
5. 68 + 82	**6.** 57 + 89	**7.** 95 + 33	**8.** 28 + 26
9. 29 + 49	**10.** 87 + 87	**11.** 33 + 27	**12.** 91 + 84
13. 84 + 56	**14.** 23 + 31	**15.** 73 + 25	**16.** 57 + 72

17. 67 + 96 = _____   **18.** 43 + 92 = _____   **19.** 37 + 98 = _____

20. 75 + 58 = _____   **21.** 25 + 91 = _____   **22.** 79 + 46 = _____

Real World Connection

Write the number sentence and solve.

23. Jan and Inez are partners in a relay race.
Jan runs the first leg of the race in 65 seconds.
Inez runs the last leg of the relay in 78 seconds.
What is their total time to run the relay?

_____

Name _____   Date _____

····· IT'S ADDING UP AT THE CAR WASH ·····

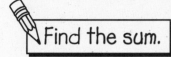

Find the sum.

1. 348 + 236	**2.** 374 + 561	**3.** 733 + 548

4. 895 + 364	**5.** 584 + 263	**6.** 475 + 650	
7. $2.33 + 3.78	**8.** $2.54 + 1.30	**9.** $7.75 + 6.80	**10.** $2.45 + 9.32
11. 325 406 + 171	**12.** 450 337 + 579	**13.** 2,537 624 + 769	**14.** 6,904 137 + 3,264
15. 98 346 297 + 16	**16.** $5.68 3.27 1.41 + 0.84	**17.** $9.83 37.64 8.39 + 1.72	**18.** $0.98 3.46 2.97 + 0.49

Real World Connection

Write the number sentence and solve.

19. Marc spent $3.89 for car wax, $1.55 for a sponge, and $2.19 for window cleaner. How much money did he spend?

_____

·········· WILD ABOUT ESTIMATING ··········

Estimate the difference by rounding.

1. 935
    − 265

2. 728
    − 333

3. 566
    − 247

4. 641
    − 258

5. 932
    − 567

6. 4,731
    − 1,545

  9,632
  5,738

8. 7,092
    − 4,666

9. $22.97
    − 13.36

10. $63.75
    − 37.32

11. 6⌄5 − 367 = _____

12. 800 − 339 = _____

13. $7⌄72 − $9.98 = _____

14. 8,157 − 4,461 = _____

Use estimation to help you circle the weight that will balance the scale.

15.

/ 733 \ / 596 ? \

/ 37 \   / 137 \   / 497 \

16.

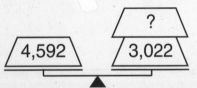

/ 4,592 \ / 3,022 ? \

/ 1,570 \   / 570 \   / 4,647 \

Real World Connection

Solve.

17. The reptile house at the zoo had 432 reptiles. Last week 185 of the reptiles were moved to another zoo. Were there *more than* or *fewer than* 200 reptiles remaining in the reptile house?

_____

Name _____ Date _____

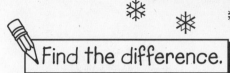
Find the difference.

1. 79 − 25	**2.** 95 − 58	**3.** 87 − 76	**4.** 73 − 56
5. 43 − 39	**6.** 98 − 67	**7.** 80 − 29	**8.** 76 − 27
9. 42 − 3	**10.** 25 − 15	**11.** 76 − 34	**12.** 61 − 26
13. 51 − 49	**14.** 59 − 35	**15.** 84 − 39	**16.** 65 − 46

17. 53 − 45 = _____ **18.** 81 − 63 = _____ **19.** 78 − 52 = _____

20. 92 − 84 = _____ **21.** 93 − 37 = _____ **22.** 67 − 42 = _____

23. 45 − 32 = _____ **24.** 68 − 49 = _____ **25.** 80 − 29 = _____

Real World Connection

Write the number sentence and solve.

26. Mr. Harrison had 54 snow shovels in his store. After a sale, 8 shovels were left. How many shovels did Mr. Harrison sell?

_____

Name _____ Date _____

•••••••••• A FAIR DIFFERENCE ••••••••••

Find the difference.

1. 517
    − 292

2. 789
    − 294

3. 793
    − 189

4. $8.37
    − 1.57

5. $6.35
    − 2.27

6. $7.26
    − 1.58

7. 4,731
    − 1,545

8. 5,789
    − 1,861

9. 9,632
    − 5,768

10. 2,739
    − 1,985

11. 6,744
    − 1,375

12. 5,837
    − 2,678

13. 806 − 257 = _____

14. 912 − 88 = _____

15. $6.34 − $5.58 = _____

16. $9.53 − $6.59 = _____

17. 8,549 − 7,234 = _____

18. 4,960 − 3,879 = _____

Real World Connection

Write the number sentence and solve.

19. On Saturday, 5,256 people rode the roller coaster. On Sunday, 4,937 people rode the roller coaster. How many more people rode the roller coaster on Saturday?

_____

•••••••••• MIXING UP MUFFINS ••••••••••

Find the sum or difference.

1. 43
  + 14

2. 78
  − 65

3. 90
  + 24

4. 97
  − 49

5. 971
  + 309

6. $9.32
  − 2.45

7. 635
  − 289

8. 8,187
  + 913

9. 4,092
  − 3,666

10. $49.60
  − 30.91

11. 6,707
  + 5,499

12. 3,569
  + 4,483

13. 70,463
  − 8,295

14. 273
  26
  + 102

15. 142 − 84 = _____

16. 76 + 41 = _____

17. $5.72 + $2.21 = _____

18. 743 − 152 = _____

19. 1,210 − 310 = _____

20. 1,805 + 2,676 = _____

Real World Connection

Write the number sentence and solve.

21. The Breakfast House makes 398 strawberry muffins. They sell 309 of them. How many strawberry muffins are left?

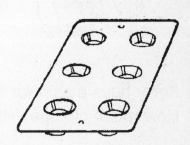

_____

Name _____   Date _____

•••• "CLOTHES" IN ON PROBLEM SOLVING ••••

Choose the strategy and solve.

1. Wendy buys an umbrella for $5 and a raincoat for $12. How much does Wendy spend on both items?

_____

2. A store takes inventory. There are 3,207 shirts and 2,831 pairs of pants in the men's department. How many pieces of clothing are there altogether in the men's department?

_____

3. On Friday, 273 customers visited the shoe store. On Saturday, 386 people visited the store. Estimate how many more people visited the store Saturday than Friday.

_____

4. The Clothes Line Boutique orders 25 blue jackets, 29 black jackets, and 32 white jackets. How many jackets does the store order in all?

_____

5. Kerry buys a shirt for $8.99 and a cap for $5.39. How much change will he get back from $20.00?

_____

TALKING ABOUT MULTIPLICATION AND DIVISION

 Write the multiplication number sentence for each array.

1.

2.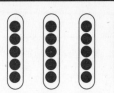

_____   _____

 Write a division number sentence for each picture.

3.

4.

5.

_____   _____   _____

_____   _____   _____

Write the three other facts for each fact family.

6. $8 \times 6 = 48$ 7. $32 \div 4 = 8$ 8. $5 \times 7 = 35$

_____   _____   _____

_____   _____   _____

_____   _____   _____

Real World Connection

Write the number sentence and solve.

9. Jill is having a party. She calls 9 people to invite them to the party. She talks to each person 3 minutes. How long does Jill spend on the phone? Write the other facts for the fact family.

_____

_____

_____

Name _____ Date _____

•••••••••••• TEAM UP ON TIMES ••••••••••••

Draw an array to solve.

1. $2 \times 6 =$ _____

2. $3 \times 8 =$ _____

Find the product.

3. 2	**4.** 2	**5.** 3	**6.** 2	**7.** 3	**8.** 3
$\times 1$	$\times 4$	$\times 1$	$\times 8$	$\times 6$	$\times 8$

9. 2	**10.** 2	**11.** 2	**12.** 3	**13.** 2	**14.** 2
$\times 9$	$\times 5$	$\times 6$	$\times 9$	$\times 7$	$\times 2$

15. 3	**16.** 2	**17.** 3	**18.** 3	**19.** 3	**20.** 3
$\times 4$	$\times 3$	$\times 5$	$\times 2$	$\times 7$	$\times 3$

21. $8 \times 3 =$ _____

22. $5 \times 3 =$ _____

23. $6 \times 2 =$ _____

24. $4 \times 2 =$ _____

25. $7 \times 3 =$ _____

26. $1 \times 3 =$ _____

Real World Connection

Write the number sentence and solve.

27. The students in Mrs. Low's class want to play tug-of-war. They would like to have 8 students on each team. How many students will they need to play the game? Write the other facts for the fact family.

_____   _____

_____   _____

Name _____ Date _____

 Draw an array to solve.

1. 4 × 5 = ____

2. 5 × 9 = ____

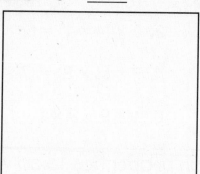

Find the product.

3. 5 × 3	**4.** 5 × 5	**5.** 4 × 1	**6.** 5 × 2	**7.** 4 × 6	**8.** 5 × 6
9. 4 × 3	**10.** 5 × 7	**11.** 4 × 8	**12.** 4 × 4	**13.** 5 × 4	**14.** 4 × 7
15. 5 × 9	**16.** 4 × 2	**17.** 5 × 1	**18.** 4 × 5	**19.** 5 × 8	**20.** 4 × 9

21. 5 × 8 = ____   **22.** 5 × 3 = ____   **23.** 5 × 7 = ____

24. 5 × 4 = ____   **25.** 4 × 7 = ____   **26.** 4 × 4 = ____

Real World Connection

Write the number sentence and solve.

27. At the boy scout campout, 4 boys sleep in each of 7 tents. How many boys are at the campout? Write the other facts for the fact family.

_____   _____

_____   _____

•••••• MULTIPLYING AT A STEADY CLIP ••••••

Write **a**, **b**, **c**, or **d** to tell which property is shown.

a. Order Property	b. Property of One	c. Zero Property	d. Grouping Property

1. $5 \times 1 = 5$ _____

2. $2 \times (4 \times 1) = (2 \times 4) \times 1$ _____

3. $8 \times 0 = 0$ _____

4. $7 \times (3 \times 2) = (7 \times 3) \times 2$ _____

5. $3 \times 4 = 4 \times 3$ _____

6. $1 \times 9 = 9 \times 1$ _____

Use the multiplication properties to solve.

7. $5 \times 7 = 35$
$7 \times 5 =$ _____

8. $9 \times 4 = 36$
$4 \times 9 =$ _____

9. $3 \times 6 = 18$
$6 \times 3 =$ _____

10. $8 \times 0 =$ _____

11. $0 \times 7 =$ _____

12. $1 \times 4 =$ _____

13. $4 \times (3 \times 2) =$ _____

14. $2 \times (1 \times 9) =$ _____

15. $3 \times (84 \times 0) =$ _____

Compare. Write <, >, or =.

16. 4×2 ◯ 9

17. 7×3 ◯ 20

18. 6×2 ◯ 2×6

19. 25 ◯ 8×3

20. $(2 \times 3) \times 3$ ◯ $2 \times (3 \times 3)$

21. 5×3 ◯ 8×2

Real World Connection

Write the number sentence and solve.

22. Beth finds 4 boxes of paper clips. She opens the boxes. All of the boxes are empty. Write a number sentence that tells the number of paper clips Beth has.

_____

Multiplication: Multiplication Properties

Math 4, SV 8048-0

• • • • • • • • • • • • • • MUSIC TIMES • • • • • • • • • • • • •

 Draw an array to solve.

1. 6 × 7 = ____

2. 7 × 4 = ____

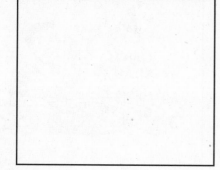

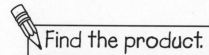 Find the product.

3.	7	4.	6	5.	7	6.	6	7.	7	8.	7
	× 6		× 1		× 0		× 7		× 2		× 4

9.	6	10.	7	11.	6	12.	5	13.	6	14.	1
	× 3		× 7		× 6		× 6		× 0		× 7

15. 6 × 8 = ____   **16.** 8 × 7 = ____   **17.** 9 × 6 = ____

18. 6 × 6 = ____   **19.** 7 × 3 = ____   **20.** 6 × 9 = ____

Real World Connection

Write the number sentence and solve.

21. Employees at the music store put new strings on 7 violins. Each violin gets 4 strings. How many strings are used?

_____

PIZZA PARTY TIMES

 Draw an array and solve.

1. $3 \times 9 =$ _____   **2.** $8 \times 8 =$ _____

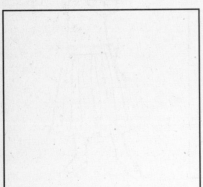

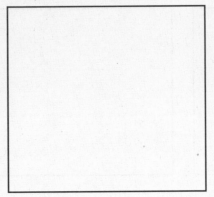

 Find the product.

3. 9 $\times 8$	**4.** 8 $\times 3$	**5.** 9 $\times 1$	**6.** 8 $\times 7$	**7.** 9 $\times 2$	**8.** 8 $\times 1$
9. 9 $\times 7$	**10.** 8 $\times 4$	**11.** 8 $\times 0$	**12.** 8 $\times 8$	**13.** 9 $\times 6$	**14.** 8 $\times 2$
15. 9 $\times 5$	**16.** 8 $\times 6$	**17.** 9 $\times 9$	**18.** 9 $\times 3$	**19.** 9 $\times 4$	**20.** 8 $\times 5$

Real World Connection

Write the number sentence and solve.

21. André orders 8 pizzas. Each pizza is cut into 6 slices. How many slices of pizza are there?

_____

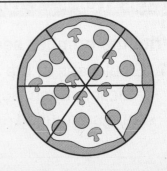

•••••••••• "EGG-STRA" PRACTICE ••••••••••

Complete each multiplication table.

Eggs

1.

x	0	1	2	3	4	5	6	7	8	9
8	0	8	16							

2.

x	0	1	2	3	4	5	6	7	8	9
7	0	7	14							

Find the product.

3. 8
  × 3

4. 9
  × 6

5. 8
  × 4

6. 3
  × 6

7. 7
  × 8

8. 5
  × 4

9. 6
  × 0

10. 4
  × 4

11. 8
  × 9

12. 4
  × 6

13. 7
  × 5

14. 9
  × 9

15. 4
  × 7

16. 5
  × 6

17. 9
  × 7

18. 4
  × 4

19. 0
  × 8

20. 7
  × 6

Find the product.

21. $8 \times 8 =$ _____

22. $7 \times 3 =$ _____

23. $8 \times 6 =$ _____

24. $6 \times 1 =$ _____

25. $4 \times 9 =$ _____

26. $9 \times 0 =$ _____

Real World Connection

Write the number sentence and solve.

27. Wanda and her dad collect 5 cartons of eggs on Tuesday. There are 6 eggs in each carton. How many eggs do Wanda and her dad collect?

_____

Name _____ Date _____

 •••••••••••••• **TIME TO SKATE** ••••••••••••••

 Write the product on the place-value chart.

Place-Value Chart			
Thousands	Hundreds	Tens	Ones

1. $2 \times 3 = 2 \times 3$ ones ⟶

$2 \times 30 = 2 \times 3$ tens ⟶

$2 \times 300 = 2 \times 3$ hundreds ⟶

$2 \times 3,000 = 2 \times 3$ thousands ⟶

 Complete each pattern.

2. $3 \times 4 =$ _____

$3 \times 40 =$ _____

$3 \times 400 =$ _____

$3 \times 4,000 =$ _____

3. $7 \times$ _____ $= 28$

$7 \times 40 =$ _____

$7 \times$ _____ $= 2,800$

$7 \times 4,000 =$ _____

Find each product.

4.

H	T	O
2	3	9
×		3

5.

T	O
4	6
×	4

6.

H	T	O
1	2	2
×		5

7.

T	O
1	9
×	8

Real World Connection

Write the number sentence and solve.

8. Julia's family pays $18 a day to roller-skate. How much will they pay for 4 days of roller-skating?

_____

Name _____ Date _____

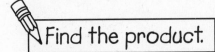
Find the product.

1. 62
× 4

2. 67
× 3

3. 41
× 6

4. 78
× 3

5. 93
× 9

6. 52
× 4

7. 12
× 8

8. 34
× 5

9. 31
× 6

10. 9 × 46 = _____

11. 2 × 47 = _____

12. 5 × 36 = _____

13. 4 × 45 = _____

14. 3 × 39 = _____

15. 3 × 72 = _____

16. 6 × 27 = _____

17. 8 × 63 = _____

18. 5 × 45 = _____

19. 4 × 33 = _____

20. 4 × 42 = _____

21. 6 × 28 = _____

Real World Connection

Write the number sentence and solve.

22. At a park work day, 26 people come to rake leaves. They each rake 4 bags of leaves. How many bags of leaves are raked?

_____

·········· IT'S TIME TO DELIVER ··········

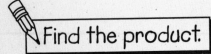

Find the product.

1. 287 × 2	2. 114 × 3	3. 317 × 3

4. 175 × 5	5. 248 × 3	6. 182 × 4

7. 385 × 2	8. 319 × 3	9. 136 × 5	10. 246 × 4

11. 328 × 6	12. 473 × 4	13. 279 × 7	14. 305 × 3

15. 2,096 × 2	16. 1,786 × 4	17. 4,365 × 3	18. 7,258 × 4

19. 3 × 318 = _____   20. 3 × 534 = _____

21. 7 × 3,624 = _____   22. 6 × 4,633 = _____

Real World Connection

Write the number sentence and solve.

23. Each delivery truck can be loaded with 1,086 newspapers. How many newspapers can be loaded onto 3 trucks?

THE TIMES

_____

Name _____ Date _____

•••••••• SHOPPING FOR PRODUCTS ••••••••

Estimate by rounding to the next higher dime, dollar, or ten dollars. Then find the product.

1. $6.38 ⟶ $7.00
   ×   3 ⟶ ×   3

2. $0.72 ⟶
   ×   9 ⟶

3. $4.52 ⟶
   ×   6 ⟶

4. $42.85 ⟶
   ×   3 ⟶

5. $15.76 ⟶
   ×   4 ⟶

6. $5.29 ⟶
   ×   4 ⟶

7. $0.82 ⟶
   ×   5 ⟶

8. $46.71 ⟶
   ×   6 ⟶

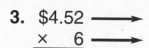 Find the product.

9. 9 × $2.94 = _____

10. 3 × $0.47 = _____

11. 8 × $1.45 = _____

12. 3 × $0.99 = _____

13. 5 × $1.61 = _____

14. 2 × $7.04 = _____

Real World Connection

Write the number sentence and solve.

15. A bakery buys 6 baskets of apples. Each basket costs $9.40. What is the cost of the apples?

Green apples
$9.40

_____

•••••••• WRITING ABOUT PRODUCTS ••••••••

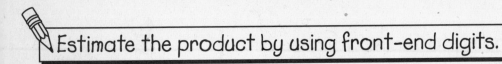

Estimate the product by using front-end digits.

U.S.
MAIL

1. 13 ⟶ 10
    × 64 ⟶ × 60

2. 48 ⟶
    × 29 ⟶

3. 63 ⟶
    × 87 ⟶

4. 32 ⟶
    × 15 ⟶

Estimate the product by rounding.

5. 14 ⟶
    × 57 ⟶

6. 39 ⟶
    × 25 ⟶

7. 61 ⟶
    × 88 ⟶

8. 28 ⟶
    × 22 ⟶

Round to the nearest dollar. Estimate the product.

9. 17 × $4.79 = _____

10. 58 × $9.09 = _____

11. 45 × $1.14 = _____

Round to the nearest ten cents. Estimate the product.

12. 22 × $3.39 = _____

13. 68 × $2.15 = _____

14. 71 × $1.09 = _____

Real World Connection

Write the number sentence and solve.

15. A mail carrier delivers mail on 18 streets each day. Each street has 56 houses. About how many houses are on the mail carrier's route?

_____

Name _____ Date _____

THE DRIVE TO FIND THE PRODUCT

Find the product.

1. 57
× 32

2. 36
× 96

3. 84
× 17

4. 62
× 45

5. 79
× 24

6. 76
× 48

7. 39
× 23

8. 90
× 75

9. 29
× 63

10. 56
× 42

11. 64
× 33

12. 59
× 32

13. 44
× 96

14. 53
× 38

15. 40 × 78 = _____

16. 42 × 57 = _____

17 26 × 43 = _____

18. 68 × 46 = _____

Real World Connection

Write the number sentence and solve.

19. Raul drives 18 miles to work. He drives home using the same route. How far does Raul drive in a 21-day work month?

_____

Name _____ Date _____

⋯⋯⋯⋯⋯ GROWING PRODUCTS ⋯⋯⋯⋯⋯

 Find the product.

1. 345
   × 12

2. 342
   × 68

3. 164
   × 53

4. 304
   × 82

5. 657
   × 89

6. 108
   × 87

7. 1,463
   × 34

8. $27.86
   × 43

9. $81.57
   × 92

10. 20,016
    × 45

11. 89 × 508 = _____

12. 62 × 258 = _____

13. 56 × 613 = _____

14. 40 × 768 = _____

15. 24 × 5,063 = _____

16. 36 × 895 = _____

Real World Connection

Write the number sentence and solve.

17. Barbara places an order with a wholesale bulb company for her flower shop. She orders 42 cartons of tulips. There are 250 bulbs in each carton. How many bulbs will Barbara get?

_____

Multiplication: Multiplying Numbers with 3 or More Digits

Math 4, SV 8048-0

Name _____   Date _____

 Find the product.

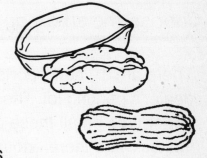

1. 8
   × 7

2. 6
   × 0

3. 15
   × 9

4. $1.37
   ×   6

5. 417
   × 8

6. 3,226
   ×   8

7. 56
   × 40

8. 32
   × 24

9. 71
   × 62

10. 372
    × 21

11. 1 × 9 = _____

12. 23 × 6 = _____

13. 300 × 4 = _____

14. 20 × 80 = _____

15. 49 × 371 = _____

16. 75 × 865 = _____

Real World Connection

Write the number sentence and solve.

17. A squirrel gathers about 37 acorns each day.
Estimate how many acorns it would gather
in 2 weeks.

_____

• • • • • • • • PROBLEM SOLVING DEALS • • • • • • • • •

Choose the strategy and solve.

1. There are 19 new sports cars sitting in the car dealer's parking lot. The manager wants to put better tires on all these cars. There are 72 tires in stock. Are there enough tires to put on all the new cars?

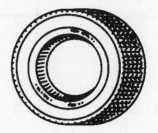

_____

2. A car dealer works 42 hours each week. How many hours does the car dealer work in one year (52 weeks)?

_____

3. The car dealership gets in a new kind of car. It can travel 36 miles on each gallon of gas. The tank can hold 18 gallons. Estimate the number of miles the car can go on a tank of gas.

_____

4. Ms. Ross earns a base pay of $1,673 per month working at a car dealership. How much does she make in one year?

_____

5. There are 7 truck sales people at Mack's Truck Town. Each sales person sells 5 trucks a week. How many trucks will be sold in 3 weeks?

_____

·····•·•·• **IT'S TIME TO DIVIDE** ·•·•·•·•·

 Write a multiplication number sentence and a division number sentence for each picture.

1.   2.

___ × ___ = ___   ___ × ___ = ___

___ ÷ ___ = ___   ___ ÷ ___ = ___

 Write the three other facts for each fact family.

3. 8 × 6 = 48   **4.** 56 ÷ 7 = 8   **5.** 6 × 7 = 42

_____   _____   _____

_____   _____   _____

 Complete. Write a number sentence to show the inverse operation.

6. 36 ÷ 4 = ____   **7.** 5 × ____ = 35   **8.** ____ × 9 = 72

_____   _____   _____

Real World Connection

Write the number sentence and solve.

9. Mrs. Panko bakes 14 cookies. She puts them into groups of 2. Then she puts the cookies into bags. How many bags of cookies does Mrs. Panko have?

Name _____   Date _____

Draw a picture to solve.

1. 9 ÷ 3 = _____

2. 12 ÷ 2 = _____

Find the quotient.

3. 27 ÷ 3 = _____   **4.** 3 ÷ 3 = _____   **5.** 18 ÷ 3 = _____

6. 4 ÷ 2 = _____   **7.** 8 ÷ 2 = _____   **8.** 21 ÷ 3 = _____

9. $2\overline{)16}$ **10.** $3\overline{)6}$ **11.** $3\overline{)27}$ **12.** $3\overline{)24}$ **13.** $2\overline{)4}$

14. $3\overline{)15}$ **15.** $3\overline{)24}$ **16.** $2\overline{)6}$ **17.** $2\overline{)10}$ **18.** $3\overline{)18}$

19. $3\overline{)12}$ **20.** $2\overline{)2}$ **21.** $2\overline{)14}$ **22.** $3\overline{)15}$ **23.** $2\overline{)18}$

Real World Connection

Write the number sentence and solve.

24. Wes and Meg find 18 sea shells. How many shells
will each get if they divide the shells evenly?

_____

Name _____ Date _____

 Draw a picture to solve.

1. 20 ÷ 4 = _____   **2.** 25 ÷ 5 = _____

 Find the quotient.

3. 40 ÷ 5 = _____   **4.** 28 ÷ 4 = _____   **5.** 15 ÷ 5 = _____

6. 32 ÷ 4 = _____   **7.** 35 ÷ 5 = _____   **8.** 16 ÷ 4 = _____

9. 4)‾20   **10.** 5)‾25   **11.** 4)‾12   **12.** 5)‾30   **13.** 5)‾45

14. 4)‾8   **15.** 5)‾5   **16.** 4)‾36   **17.** 4)‾24   **18.** 5)‾25

19. 5)‾35   **20.** 4)‾16   **21.** 5)‾15   **22.** 2)‾8   **23.** 4)‾4

Real World Connection

Write the number sentence and solve.

24. The pet shop has 24 bags of dog food. If 4 bags are used each day, how many days will the dog food last?

_____

Name _____ Date _____

•••••••••• 3, 2, 1, 0 BLAST OFF! ••••••••••

Find the quotient.

1. $0 \div 7 =$ ____   **2.** $3 \div 3 =$ ____

3. $9 \div 9 =$ ____   **4.** $0 \div 4 =$ ____

5. $18 \div 1 =$ ____   **6.** $5 \div 5 =$ ____   **7.** $64 \div 1 =$ ____

8. $7 \div 1 =$ ____   **9.** $0 \div 15 =$ ____   **10.** $8 \div 8 =$ ____

11. $17 \div 1 =$ ____   **12.** $0 \div 6 =$ ____   **13.** $14 \div 14 =$ ____

14. $4\overline{)4}$ **15.** $2\overline{)0}$ **16.** $7\overline{)7}$

17. $1\overline{)3}$ **18.** $1\overline{)1}$ **19.** $6\overline{)6}$

20. $9\overline{)0}$ **21.** $5\overline{)5}$ **22.** $1\overline{)24}$

23. $1\overline{)8}$ **24.** $14\overline{)0}$ **25.** $8\overline{)8}$

26. $1\overline{)0}$ **27.** $1\overline{)10}$ **28.** $32\overline{)32}$

Real World Connection

Write the number sentence and solve.

29. Seven children visit the space center. The tour guide has 7 pins to give the students. How many pins will each student get?

_____

Name _____ Date _____

•••••••••• EXPRESSLY DIVISION ••••••••••

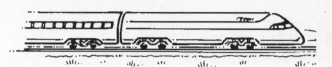

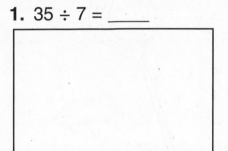 Draw a picture to solve.

1. 35 ÷ 7 = _____

2. 36 ÷ 6 = _____

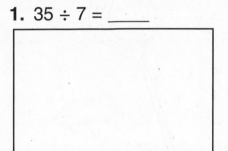 Find the quotient.

3. 14 ÷ 7 = _____   **4.** 42 ÷ 6 = _____   **5.** 18 ÷ 6 = _____

6. 63 ÷ 7 = _____   **7.** 30 ÷ 6 = _____   **8.** 54 ÷ 6 = _____

9. 6)‾24   **10.** 7)‾28   **11.** 6)‾12   **12.** 7)‾49   **13.** 6)‾6

14. 7)‾56   **15.** 7)‾21   **16.** 7)‾7   **17.** 7)‾42   **18.** 6)‾48

19. 6)‾42   **20.** 6)‾30   **21.** 7)‾14   **22.** 6)‾0   **23.** 3)‾18

Real World Connection

Write the number sentence and solve.

24. The express train makes 24 trips each day. The train runs for 6 hours. It makes the same number of trips each hour. How many trips does the train make each hour?

_____

Name _____ Date _____

 ······ **A ROSY OUTLOOK FOR DIVISION** ······

Draw a picture to solve.

1. $36 \div 9 =$ _____

2. $40 \div 8 =$ _____

Find the quotient.

3. $56 \div 8 =$ _____   **4.** $18 \div 9 =$ _____   **5.** $24 \div 8 =$ _____

6. $63 \div 9 =$ _____   **7.** $32 \div 8 =$ _____   **8.** $8 \div 8 =$ _____

9. $9\overline{)54}$ **10.** $8\overline{)64}$ **11.** $8\overline{)48}$ **12.** $9\overline{)72}$ **13.** $9\overline{)9}$

14. $8\overline{)16}$ **15.** $9\overline{)81}$ **16.** $9\overline{)27}$ **17.** $8\overline{)24}$ **18.** $8\overline{)56}$

19. $9\overline{)18}$ **20.** $8\overline{)32}$ **21.** $9\overline{)45}$ **22.** $8\overline{)0}$ **23.** $8\overline{)72}$

Real World Connection

Write the number sentence and solve.

24. The florist uses 56 roses to make 8 bouquets.
The same number of roses are in each bouquet.
How many roses are in each bouquet?

_____

•••••••• DRAWN TO DIVISION ••••••••

Find the quotient.

1. $6\overline{)42}$ **2.** $8\overline{)0}$ **3.** $4\overline{)16}$

4. $7\overline{)63}$ **5.** $6\overline{)30}$ **6.** $7\overline{)28}$

7. $9\overline{)81}$ **8.** $5\overline{)35}$ **9.** $6\overline{)24}$

10. $9\overline{)72}$ **11.** $4\overline{)16}$ **12.** $4\overline{)20}$

13. $56 \div 8 =$ _____   **14.** $18 \div 6 =$ _____   **15.** $32 \div 4 =$ _____

16. $54 \div 6 =$ _____   **17.** $24 \div 3 =$ _____   **18.** $9 \div 9 =$ _____

19. $49 \div 7 =$ _____   **20.** $64 \div 8 =$ _____   **21.** $21 \div 3 =$ _____

22. $48 \div 6 =$ _____   **23.** $36 \div 9 =$ _____   **24.** $25 \div 5 =$ _____

Real World Connection

Write the number sentence and solve.

25. Marta buys a 72-count package of paper. She divides the paper into 9 equal groups to make picture books. How many pieces of paper will be in each book?

_____

     Math 4, SV 8048-0

Name _____ Date _____

··········· DIVISION BY THE BOOK ···········

| Write how many digits there will be in each quotient. |

1. 4)800   **2.** 3)9,000   **3.** 8)40   **4.** 6)1,800

_____   _____   _____   _____

| Complete the pattern. |

5. 6)24   6)240   6)2,400

6. 9)27   9)270   9)2,700

7. 5)40   5)400   5)4,000

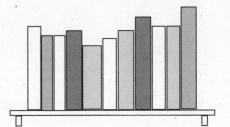

| Find the quotient. Then continue each example by changing the dividend, using multiples of 10, 100, and 1,000 to make a pattern. |

8. 4)28   **9.** 6)48   **10.** 5)45   **11.** 7)35

4)280   6)480   5)450   7)350

4)2,800   6)4,800   5)4,500   7)3,500

4)28,000   6)48,000   5)45,000   7)35,000

Real World Connection

Write the number sentence and solve.

12. The public library has 1,200 books to sell at a sale. An equal number of books are placed into 6 bookcases. How many books are in each bookcase?

_____

Division: Dividends with Multiples of Tens

                   Math 4, SV 8048-0

Name _____   Date _____

Find the quotient using the models.

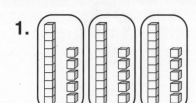

1. $3\overline{)45}$

2. $2\overline{)48}$

Use place-value blocks to find the quotient.

3. $3\overline{)69}$ **4.** $2\overline{)26}$ **5.** $4\overline{)84}$ **6.** $2\overline{)36}$

7. $2\overline{)30}$ **8.** $4\overline{)52}$ **9.** $5\overline{)55}$ **10.** $2\overline{)54}$

11. $72 \div 3 =$ _____   **12.** $75 \div 5 =$ _____   **13.** $42 \div 3 =$ _____

14. $48 \div 3 =$ _____   **15.** $72 \div 6 =$ _____   **16.** $56 \div 4 =$ _____

Real World Connection

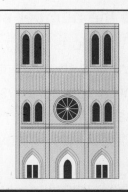

Write the number sentence and solve.

17. There are 64 students taking a tour of a cathedral.
The students will be broken into 4 equal groups.
How many students will be in each tour group?

_____

• • • • • • • • • • • • • • • WHAT IS LEFT? • • • • • • • • • • • • • •

Write an **X** where the first digit in the quotient should be placed.

1. 6)30   2. 5)84   3. 9)75   4. 3)82

Find the quotient. Check by multiplying.

5. 3)51 Check: 6. 4)55 Check: 7. 6)82 Check:

8. 4)96 Check: 9. 4)87 Check: 10. 5)65 Check:

11. 3)89 Check: 12. 6)71 Check: 13. 8)58 Check:

Real World Connection

Write the number sentence and solve.

4. Ricardo is making club sandwiches for his party. Each sandwich needs 3 slices of bread. The loaf of bread he buys has 52 slices in it. How many sandwiches can Ricardo make? If he has extra slices, how many will he have?

_____

Name _____   Date _____

Circle the letter of the best estimate. Write the method you used.

1. 3)175   **a.** 50   **b.** 60   **c.** 70   **d.** 75   _____

2. 4)243   **a.** 40   **b.** 70   **c.** 60   **d.** 80   _____

3. 2)178   **a.** 90   **b.** 80   **c.** 75   **d.** 78   _____

Estimate the quotient. Look for compatible numbers.

4. 2)107   **5.** 3)185   **6.** 4)158   **7.** 8)235   **8.** 7)148

9. 3)208   **10.** 5)403   **11.** 6)131   **12.** 4)321   **13.** 2)165

14. 275 ÷ 9 = _____   **15.** 426 ÷ 7 = _____   **16.** 356 ÷ 6 = _____

17. 555 ÷ 8 = _____   **18.** 809 ÷ 9 = _____   **19.** 348 ÷ 5 = _____

Real World Connection

Write the number sentence and solve.

20. A theater has 238 seats. The seats are arranged in 3 sections of the same size. About how many seats are in each section?

_____

Name _____ Date _____

 Write an **x** where the first digit in the quotient should be placed.

1. 4)348   **2.** 5)712   **3.** 7)948   **4.** 4)678

 Find the quotient. Check by multiplying.

5. 3)254   Check: **6.** 2)130   Check: **7.** 6)737   Check:

8. 5)419   Check: **9.** 3)167   Check: **10.** 6)487   Check:

11. 3)841   Check: **12.** 4)573   Check: **13.** 4)360   Check:

Real World Connection

Write the number sentence and solve.

14. Gary works in a music store. He arranges 875 compact discs equally on 9 shelves. How many compact discs fit on each shelf?

Wrap Music CD

_____

Name _____   Date _____

• • • • • • • • • • • ACROSS THE BRIDGE • • • • • • • • • • • •

Write an **x** where the first digit in the quotient should be placed.

1. 4)216   2. 8)578   3. 5)602   4. 8)824

Estimate. Then find the quotient.

5. 7)722   Estimate: _____   6. 4)809   Estimate: _____   7. 8)859   Estimate: _____

8. 3)617   Estimate: _____   9. 2)612   Estimate: _____   10. 5)534   Estimate: _____

Complete. Use mental math to find **n**.

11. If $600 \div 6 = 100$,
then $602 \div 6 = n$.

$n =$ _____

12. If $300 \div 3 = 100$,
then $301 \div 3 = n$.

$n =$ _____

13. If $800 \div 4 = 200$,
then $803 \div 4 = n$.

$n =$ _____

Real World Connection

Write the number sentence and solve.

14. In a traffic survey, the transportation department counts the number of vehicles crossing the West Side Bridge. They find that in 4 hours, 812 cars cross this bridge. What is the average number of cars which cross the West Side Bridge per hour?

_____

Name _____   Date _____

• • • • • • • • • • • CHECK THE RECEIPT • • • • • • • • • •

Find the quotient. Check by multiplying.

Hamburger $2

French Fries $1

Hot dog $1.50

Soda   S $1.00
          L $1.50

1. 3)$2.79   Check   **2.** 5)$8.50   Check:

3. 4)$8.16   Check: **4.** 6)$5.22   Check:

5. 8)$6.32   Check: **6.** 5)$6.00   Check: **7.** 7)$9.10   Check

8. $8.14 ÷ 2 = _____   **9.** $5.44 ÷ 8 = _____   **10.** $8.05 ÷ 7 = _____

Check: Check: Check:

Real World Connection

Write the number sentence and solve.

11. Spudhouse has a special offer of 2 dinners for $9.72. How much is one dinner?

_____

•••••••••• CONQUER AND DIVIDE ••••••••••

Record each quotient in the place-value chart.

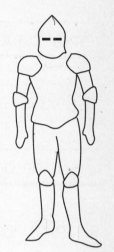

Place-Value Chart	
Tens	Ones

1. 4)24

40)240

40)2,400

Place-Value Chart	
Tens	Ones

2. 6)54

60)540

60)5,400

Place-Value Chart	
Tens	Ones

3. 8)40

80)400

80)4,000

Place-Value Chart	
Tens	Ones

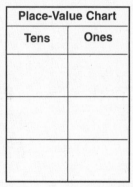

4. 7)56

70)560

700)5,600

Write the basic fact that helps you find each quotient. Solve.

5. 30)120 fact: _____

6. 20)160 fact: _____

7. 40)280 fact: _____

8. 50)300 fact: _____

Real World Connection

Write the number sentence and solve.

9. Megan read a 160-page book about castles and the people living at that time period. She read 40 pages each day. How many days did it take Megan to read the book?

_____

Division: Dividing by Multiples of ___

Math 4, SV 80___-0

• • • • • • • • • • • • • • • **A-TEN-TION!** • • • • • • • • • • • • • •

Write an **x** where the first digit in the quotient should be placed.

1. 60)365   **2.** 40)250   **3.** 70)295   **4.** 90)189

Find the quotient. Check by multiplying.

5. 30)68   Check: **6.** 20)88   Check: **7.** 60)331   Check:

8. 50)268   Check: **9.** 40)295   Check: **10.** 80)500   Check:

11. 50)475   Check: **12.** 30)161   Check: **13.** 40)227   Check:

Real World Connection

Write the number sentence and solve.

14. There are 190 people in a marching band. The band director wants to put the band members into rows of 20. How many full rows will there be? How many extra people will be in one row?

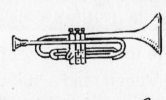

_____

Name _____ Date _____

····· HORSING AROUND WITH DIVISION ·····

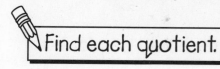

Find each quotient.

1. $12\overline{)49}$

2. $24\overline{)98}$

3. $31\overline{)94}$

4. $20\overline{)67}$

5. $21\overline{)108}$

6. $42\overline{)169}$

7. $90\overline{)237}$

8. $85\overline{)425}$

9. $72\overline{)377}$

10. $63\overline{)260}$

11. $19\overline{)143}$

12. $47\overline{)255}$

13. $32\overline{)224}$

14. $52\overline{)321}$

Real World Connection

Write a number sentence and solve.

15. There are 23 horses at the Rocky Creek Ranch. There are 115 children staying at the camp for the week. How many trail rides will the horses need to take so that all the children can ride one time?

_____

Name _____   Date _____

Write an **x** where the first digit in the quotient should be placed.

1. $43\overline{)567}$ **2.** $29\overline{)304}$ **3.** $17\overline{)249}$ **4.** $63\overline{)495}$

Estimate. Then find the quotient.

5. Estimate _____   **6.** Estimate _____   **7.** Estimate _____

$43\overline{)97}$ $67\overline{)250}$ $32\overline{)135}$

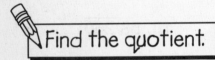

Find the quotient.

8. $28\overline{)793}$ **9.** $36\overline{)582}$ **10.** $70\overline{)856}$ **11.** $42\overline{)652}$

12. $\$17\overline{)\$612}$ **13.** $\$34\overline{)\$204}$ **14.** $\$14\overline{)\$322}$ **15.** $\$39\overline{)\$468}$

Real World Connection

Write the number sentence and solve.

16. The city park is sponsoring a cleanup day. There
are 204 volunteers. They are divided into 17
teams. How many people work on each team?

_____

Name _____ Date _____

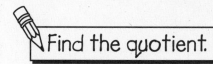 Find the quotient.

1. 8)56　　　　2. 6)40　　　　3. 15)67

4. 42)84　　　　5. 3)215　　　　6. 40)800

7. 7)644　　　　8. 8)$6.32　　　　9. 3)258　　　　10. 32)241

11. 81 ÷ 9 = ____　　　12. 52 ÷ 4 = ____　　　13. 48 ÷ 3 = ____

14. 68 ÷ 30 = ____　　　15. 450 ÷ 5 = ____　　　16. 126 ÷ 21 = ____

Real World Connection

Write the number sentence and solve.

17. The River City Orchestra practices a total of 64 hours each month. If they practice 4 hours each day, how many days does the orchestra practice each month?

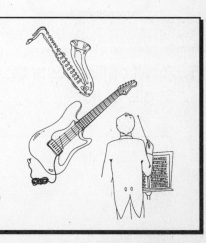

_____

Math 4, SV 8048-0

•• DEVELOPING PROBLEM SOLVING SKILLS ••

| Choose the strategy and solve. |

1. Mr. Topaz is a school portrait photographer. He can photograph 527 students in 5 hours. Estimate about how many students he photographs each hour.

_____

2. Marian has 106 photographs to put in a new album. Each page holds 16 photographs. How many photographs will there be on the last page?

_____

3. Hans earns $689 as a photographer. He gets a paycheck after working 13 days. How much money does Hans earn each day?

_____

4. Jennifer wants to buy a camera that costs $123. She saves $8 per week. In how many weeks will Jennifer have enough to buy the camera?

_____

5. A roll of film costs $2.49. Is $10.00 enough to buy 5 rolls of film?

_____

• • • • • • • • • • • • *TIME FOR WORK* • • • • • • • • • • • • •

Write the time in two different ways.

1.

_____

_____

2.

_____

_____

3.

_____

_____

4.

_____

_____

 Match the time with the clock.

5. four minutes past six

6. twenty-three minutes to eight

```
6:04
```

```
7:37
```

Real World Connection

Solve.

7. Jim preheated the oven at 3:00. Jason prepared the bread dough at 2:50. Helen put some rolls in the oven at quarter past three. Which activity took place first?

_____

Time and Graphs: Telling Time

•••••••••••••• **YOUR TIME IS UP** ••••••••••••

 Choose the most reasonable unit of time for each:
second, minute, hour, day, week, month, or year.

1. Summer lasts about 3 _____ .

2. It takes about 10 _____
   to take a shower.

3. To eat your breakfast
   takes about 20 _____ .

4. It takes about one _____
   to tear paper.

Choose the best estimate for each.

5. The time it takes
   to set up a tent.

   a. 15 minutes

   b. 5 hours

   c. 5 days

6. The time it takes
   to get a good night's sleep.

   a. 8 seconds

   b. 80 minutes

   c. 8 hours

Real World Connection

Solve.

7. Jeff thought his piano lesson would last about one
   hour. His lesson started at 2:55 P.M. About what
   time will his lesson be over?

_____

• • • • • • • • • • • • • • **TIME TO BEGIN** • • • • • • • • • • • • •

Tell how much time has elapsed.

1.

Begin A.M.   End P.M.

_____

2.

Begin A.M.   End P.M.

_____

Use the clocks to help you answer Exercises 3-5.

3. How many minutes pass from 1:20 P.M. to 1:55 P.M.?

4. How many hours pass from 9:00 A.M. to 2:00 P.M.?

5. What is the time when it is 30 minutes before 8:15 A.M.?

_____   _____   _____

Real World Connection

Solve.

6. Luis went outside to ride his bike at 3:35 P.M. His mother told him to be home by 4:10 P.M. How long did Luis have to ride his bike?

_____

Time and Graphs: Elapsed Time

Math 4, SV 8048-0

Name _____   Date _____

DAYS OF SPRING

Use the calendar to answer Exercises 1-3.

✿ ✿ ✿ **MAY** ✿ ✿ ✿						
Sun	Mon	Tues	Wed	Thurs	Fri	Sat
		1	2	3	4	5
6	7	8	9	10	11	12
13	14	15	16	17	18	19
20	21	22	23	24	25	26
27	28	29	30	31		

1. Write the date of the first Sunday.   _____

2. Write the date of the second Monday.   _____

3. Write the date one week before May 24.   _____

Write the day and date. Use the May calendar.

4. 4 days after May 21.   5. The third Friday in May.

_____   _____

Real World Connection

Solve.

6. John goes to the spring festival on Friday, May 11. Lisa leaves 3 days later. On what day and date does Lisa leave?

_____

Name _____   Date _____

THE SPORTS LINES ・・・・・・・・・・・

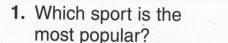
Use this tally table to answer Exercises 1–4.

1. Which sport is the most popular? _____

2. How many people like basketball or football? _____

3. How many people participated in this survey? _____

4. Complete the frequency column.

Favorite Sports		
Sport	Tally	Frequency
Soccer	ⲧⲏⲕ̶ I	
Tennis	IIII	
Swimming	ⲧⲏⲕ̶ III	
Basketball	ⲧⲏⲕ̶ ⲧⲏⲕ̶ ⲧⲏⲕ̶	
Football	ⲧⲏⲕ̶ IIII	

Use the frequency table to answer Exercises 5–7.

5. How many more visitors attended Game 3 than Game 4?

_____

6. To which game did the least number of visitors come?

_____

7. List the games in order from greatest attendance to least attendance.

_____

Center School Soccer Team Number of Visitors at Home Games	
Game	Frequency
Game 1	140
Game 2	195
Game 3	182
Game 4	108
Game 5	220

Real World Connection

Solve.

8. Take a survey of at least ten people to find their favorite sport. Make a frequency table from your tallies.

Favorite Sports		
Sport	Tally	Frequency

www.svschoolsupply.com

© Steck-Vaughn Company

Time and Graphs: Collecting Data

Math 4, SV 8048-0

Name _____ Date _____

•••••••••••••• PICTURE THIS ••••••••••••••

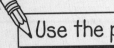

Use the pictograph to answer Exercises 1-3.

Number of Shirts Sold	
Monday	👕👕👕👕👕👕
Tuesday	👕👕👕👕
Wednesday	👕👕
Thursday	👕👕👕
Friday	👕👕👕👕👕👕👕
Key: Each 👕 stands for 10 shirts.	

1. On which day were the fewest shirts sold? _____

2. Were more shirts sold on Tuesday or Wednesday? _____

3. How many shirts were sold on Wednesday? ___ Friday? ___ Monday? ___

Use the pictograph to answer Exercises 4-5.

Boxes of Buttons Used	
Monday	⚪⚪⚪⚪⚪⚪⚪
Tuesday	⚪⚪⚪⚪
Wednesday	⚪⚪
Thursday	⚪⚪⚪
Friday	⚪⚪⚪⚪
Key: Each ⚪ stands for 20 boxes of buttons.	

4. How many more boxes of buttons were used on Monday than on Thursday? _____

5. How many boxes of buttons did they use all five days? _____

Real World Connection

Solve.

6. Take a survey of at least ten people to see what kind of shirt they are wearing. Complete the pictograph.

Kinds of Shirts	
T-shirt	
Shirt with Buttons	
Other	
Key: Each 👕 stands for 1 shirt.	

Name _____ Date _____

The art teacher asked students which art project they wanted to work on. A bar graph shows the results. Use this graph to answer Exercises 1–5.

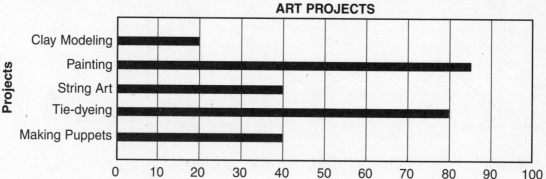

ART PROJECTS

Projects: Clay Modeling, Painting, String Art, Tie-dyeing, Making Puppets

Scale: 0 10 20 30 40 50 60 70 80 90 100

1. Is this a vertical bar graph or a horizontal bar graph? _____

2. What do the numbers below the graph show? _____

3. What does each interval of the scale represent? _____

4. Which project was most popular? _____

5. Which project was least popular? _____

Real World Connection

Solve.

6. Use the table to complete the bar graph. Remember:
   • Choose a scale.
   • Label the graph.
   • Write a title for the graph.

Lawns Mowed This Summer	
Name	**Number**
Will	6
Taylor	10
Joaquin	8
Barb	4

Name _____ Date _____

GET IN LINE

Use the graph to answer Exercises 1-3.

The theater made a line graph to show the number of sales for six days.

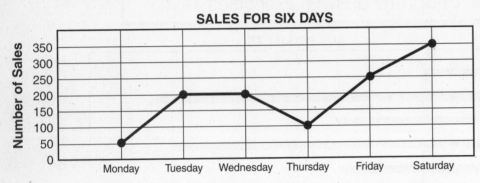

SALES FOR SIX DAYS

1. During which day was the number of sales greatest? _____

2. During which day was the number of sales least? _____

3. How many sales were there on

   Wednesday? _____ Friday? _____ Monday? _____

Real World Connection

Solve.

4. The table shows the average temperatures for October through March in Miami, Florida. Complete the line graph to show how the temperature changed.

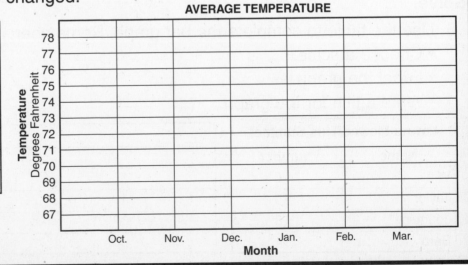

Month	Average Temperature
October	78˚F
November	72˚F
December	68˚F
January	67˚F
February	68˚F
March	71˚F

AVERAGE TEMPERATURE

Name _____ Date _____

Use the grid to answer Exercises 1-12.

Write the letter for each point.

1. (4,2) _____ **2.** (9,6) _____

3. (2,1) _____ **4.** (8,7) _____

5. (6,4) _____ **6.** (10,8) _____

Write the ordered pair for each letter.

7. A _____ **8.** V _____

9. N _____ **10.** E _____

11. F _____ **12.** I _____

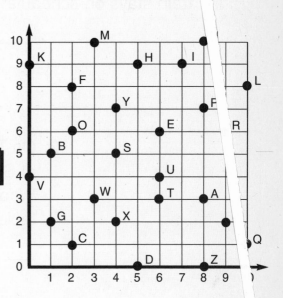

Use the letters at the points to solve the riddle.
Move right and up to find each letter.

13. What does a leopard say when it rains?

(6,3) (5,9) (8,3) (6,3)   (5,9) (7,9) (6,3) (4,5)

(6,3) (5,9) (6,6)   (4,5) (8,7) (2,6) (6,3)

_____

Real World Connection

Solve.

14. Think of a word. Use ordered pairs to spell out
your word. Have your partner find your word.

_____

Name _____   Date _____

Choose the strategy and solve. Use the train schedule to help you.

1. What time will Train A stop in Woodruff if the train stays on schedule?

_____

Train Schedule for Weekdays			
Station	**Train A** **A.M.**	**Train B** **A.M.**	**Train C** **P.M.**
Edison	7:12	9:00	12:10
Sunset	7:27	9:20	12:25
Fairfax	7:42	9:40	12:50
Woodruff	———	10:00	1:02
Linden	8:12	10:20	1:20
Layton	8:37	10:40	1:53

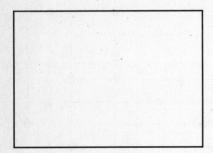

2. On Train C, 34 people get on at Edison, 24 get on at Sunset, 16 get on at Fairfax, and 30 get on at Woodruff. Using these frequencies, make a tally table to show the data.

_____

3. Using the table in Exercise 2, draw any kind of graph to show the data.

_____

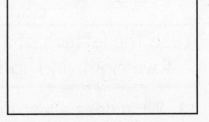

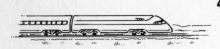

4. How many people get on Train C according to the data?

_____

5. Beginning on August 9, Meisha rides the train to work for three days. On week days, her ticket costs $6. It doubles on weekend days. How much does Meisha spend on tickets for the three days?

_____

August						
Sun	Mon	Tues	Wed	Thur	Fri	Sat
			1	2	3	4
5	6	7	8	9	10	11
12	13	14	15	16	17	18
19	20	21	22	23	24	25
26	27	28	29	30	31	

Name _____ Date _____

•••••••••• DOES IT MEASURE UP? ••••••••••

INCHES	1	2	3	4	5

Use a Ruler. Find the length of each object in centimeters and in inches. Record your measurements.

	Object	Centimeters	Inches
1.	a marker		
2.	a crayon		
3.	a paper clip		
4.	height of your chair		
5.	a folder		
6.	a chalkboard eraser		
7.	a calculator		

8. Use a ruler to draw a rectangle.
The length should be 3 inches.
The width should be centimeters.

Real World Connection

Solve.

9. Lee wants to make a picture frame with wood. She needs 96 inches of framing. Lee has two inch strips of wood. Does she have enough wood for the frame? Explain your answer.

_____

_____

•••••••••••• **GOING THE DISTANCE** ••••••••••••

Choose the appropriate unit for each. Write **inches**, **feet**, **yards**, or **miles**.

1. The length of an envelope is about 9 _____.

2. The height of a street lamp is about 9 _____.

3. The length of a ramp is about 3 _____.

4. The height of a mountain is about 9, 257 _____.

Circle the longer unit.

5. 3 ft or 3 yd   6. 16 ft or 16 in   7. 23 mi or 23 yd   8. 400 in or 400 yd

Use the table for Exercises 9–10.

9. Which river is longer than 2,000 miles?

_____

10. How long is Snake River?

_____

Lengths of U.S. Rivers	
River	**Length in Miles**
Ohio	1,310
Copper	286
Snake	1,040
Mississippi	2,340
Tennessee	886

Real World Connection

Solve.

11. Lana lives in Clarkville. She wants to go to Clear Valley by the shortest route. Will she go through Bruster or Capital City? Explain your answer.

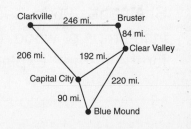

_____

_____

• • • • • • • • • • • IN THE KITCHEN • • • • • • • • • • •

Choose the appropriate unit of measure. Write _teaspoon_, _tablespoon_, _cup_, _pint_, _quart_, or _gallon_.

1.
_____

2.
_____

3.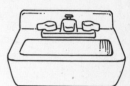
_____

4.
_____

5.
_____

6.
_____

Circle the larger unit.

7. 2 t or 2 tbsp

8. 4 pt or 4 c

9. 10 gal or 10 qt

Change each sentence so it makes sense.

10. Ellie uses 4 teaspoons of oatmeal to make cookies.

_____

11. Regan pours a gallon of milk in his glass.

_____

Real World Connection

Solve.

12. José pours 1 cup of apple juice and 3 cups of grape juice into a large bottle. How many pints of juice are in the bottle?

_____

Math 4, SV 8048-0

• • • • • • • • • • • • • • • **WEIGHING IN** • • • • • • • • • • • • • • •

Choose the appropriate unit to measure. Write **ounce**, **pound**, or **ton**.

1.

_____

2.

_____

3.

_____

4.

_____

5.

_____

6.

_____

Circle the more reasonable measurement.

7.

1 oz or 1 lb

8.

7 lb or 70 lb

9.

5 oz or 25 oz

Complete. You may use a calculator.

10. 5 lb = _____ oz   **11.** 13 T = _____ lb   **12.** 64 oz = _____ lb

Real World Connection

Solve.

13. Rose's family recipe for muffins calls for 12 ounces of chopped apples to serve 4 people. How many pounds of chopped apples should Rose add to the batter to serve 16 people?

_____

Measurement: Customary Units of Weight

Math 4, SV 8048-0

Name _____ Date _____

 Circle the more reasonable answer.

1.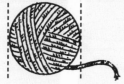

a. 2 cm   b. 20 cm

2.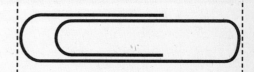

a. 6 dm   b. 6 cm

3.

a. 1 dm   b. 10 dm

 Choose the appropriate unit for each. Write **centimeter**, **decimeter**, **meter**, or **kilometer**.

4. height of your desk _____

5. height of a flag pole _____

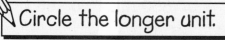

6. length of a road _____

7. length of a calculator _____

 Circle the longer unit.

8. 5 cm or 5 dm   9. 10 m or 10 dm   10. 16 km or 16 dm   11. 2 m or 2 cm

Real World Connection

Write the number sentence and solve.

12. Enrique swims 7 km a day for 1 week. How many km does he swim in that period of time?

_____

Name _____   Da_ _____

MEASURE IN METRIC

Choose the appropriate unit of measure. Write *milliliters* or *liters*.

1. a large jug of water _____

2.  a bowl of soup _____

3.  water in a pool _____

4. a small glass of juice _____

Circle the correct measure.

5.

1 mL or 1 L

6.

500 mL or 500 L

7.

12__ mL or 120 L

Circle the most reasonable measurement.

8. A water cooler holds about ____. **a.** 4 mL   **b.** 40 mL   **c.** 4 L

9. A jar of honey holds about ____. **a.** 65 mL   **b.** 650 m   **c.** 65 L

10. A milk carton holds about ____. **a.** 20 mL   **b.** 2 L   **c.** 20 L

Real World Connection

Solve.

11. A tall vase holds about 2 L of water. A wide vase holds about 2,300 mL of water. Which holds more?

_____

• • • • • • • • • • • MADE TO MEASURE • • • • • • • • • • •

 Choose the appropriate unit to weigh each item.
Write **grams** or **kilograms**.

1.
_____

2.
_____

3.
_____

4.
_____

5.
_____

6.
_____

 Circle the more reasonable measurement.

7.

a feather

1 g or 100 g

8.

a truck

175 kg or 1,750 kg

9.

a pair of gloves

20 g or 200 g

10.

a piano

40 kg or 450 kg

Real World Connection

Write the number sentence and solve.

11. Karen needs 1 kilogram of flour. She has 275
grams. How much more flour does Karen need?

FLOUR

_____

Name _____   Date _____

Choose the strategy and solve.

1. Jamil has an 8-foot board. Can he cut 4 lengths that are each 24 inches long?

   _____

2. Mr. Burns is painting his living room. He mixes 2 pints of red paint, 1 quart of blue paint, and 2 quarts of white paint. How many gallons of paint does Mr. Burns have?

   _____

3. Beth buys equal parts of 4 kinds of nails. The total weight of the nails is 2 pounds. How many ounces of each kind of nail does Beth buy?

   _____

4. A large cooler provides 4 workers with 1,000 mL of water each. How many liters of water does the cooler hold?

   _____

5. Joel needs to repair a second story window that is 10 meters above ground. His ladder is 2 meters long when folded, but can reach 3 times that distance when unfolded. Will his ladder reach the window?

   _____

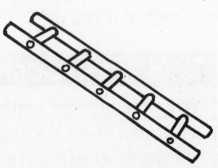

Name _____ Date _____

• • • • • • • • • • • THE PLANE TRUTH • • • • • • • • • • • •

 Write whether each is a picture of a plane figure or a solid figure.

1.   2.   3.   4.

_____ _____ _____ _____

Name the solid figure represented by each.

5.   6.   7.   8.

_____ _____ _____ _____

9.  10.   11.   12.

_____ _____ _____ _____

Real World Connection

Solve.

13. Nadia traces each side of this block.
    What plane shapes will she see?

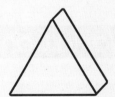

_____

_____

Name _____ Date _____

 Identify each figure. Write *line segment*, *line*, *point*, or *ray*.

1. •————•   **2.** •———→   **3.** •   **4.** ←———→

_____   _____   _____   _____

Draw each figure.

5. line AB   **6.** ray CD   **7.** line segment EF

Decide whether the figure is a line segment. Write **yes** or **no**.

8. ———→   **9.** •———•   **10.** ←———→   **11.** ◯

_____   _____   _____   _____

For Exercises 12–13, use the drawing.

12. Name 2 rays.   **13.** Name 2 lines.

_____   _____

_____   _____

Real World Connection

Solve.

14. What figure is formed inside the polygon if all of the possible line segments are drawn to connect the five points shown?

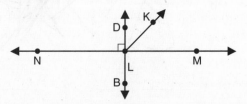

_____

•••••••• LOOKING FOR THE ANGLE ••••••••

 Write whether each example is a *right*, an *acute*, or an *obtuse* angle.

1.

_____

2.

_____

3.

_____

4.

_____

5.

_____

6.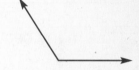

_____

7.

_____

8.

_____

9.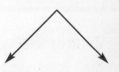

_____

 Find the number of acute angles in each.

10. **A**   11. **X**   12. **M**   13. **Y**

_____   _____   _____   _____

Real World Connection

Solve.

14. Zoo workers begin feeding the animals at 4:30 each afternoon. What kind of angle is formed inside the two clock hands?

_____

•••••••••• CIRCLE AROUND ••••••••••

For Exercises 1–3, use the circle drawing.

Use your centimeter ruler to measure the radius and the diameter.

1. Label the points on the circle.

   _____

2. How many centimeters long is the radius?

   _____

3. How many centimeters long is the diameter?

   _____

Use the drawing for Exercises 4–6.

Name the center of this circle. _____

5. Name a radius. _____

6. Name a diameter. _____

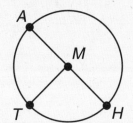

Complete. Use the drawing for Exercises 7–11.

7. Line segment *FT* is a _____ .

8. The center of the circle is _____ .

9. Line segment *AS* is a _____ .

10. Points ___ and *Y* are endpoints of a _____ .

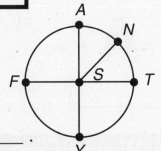

Real World Connection

Solve.

11. Miguel cuts a round pizza into 4 equal slices. What kind of angles are formed?

    _____

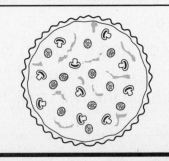

Name _____ Date _____

 Write a multiplication sentence to find the volume of each.

1.
4 cm
2 cm   3 cm

_____

_____

2.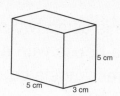
5 cm
5 cm   3 cm

_____

_____

3.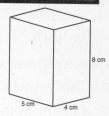
8 cm
5 cm   4 cm

_____

_____

4.
1 cm
7 cm   6 cm

_____

_____

5.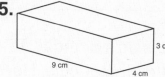
3 cm
9 cm   4 cm

_____

_____

6.
6 cm
5 cm   2 cm

_____

_____

 Complete this table for rectangular prisms.

	Length	Width	Height	Volume
7.	2 cm	4 cm	8 cm	
8.	3 cm	5 cm	2 cm	
9.	8 cm	3 cm	1 cm	
10.	4 cm		2 cm	24 cubic cm
11.		4 cm	4 cm	96 cubic cm

Real World Connection

Write the number sentence and solve.

12. Ronald is filling his fish tank. The tank measures 13 inches by 9 inches by 9 inches. What is the volume of water the tank will hold?

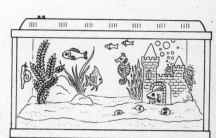

_____

···· BUILDING PROBLEM SOLVING SKILLS ····

Choose the strategy and solve.

1. For a school project, Angela is using two solid figures to make a model of a house with a roof. Write the names of the figures Angela could use on the lines below.

_____

_____

2. It is Jo's birthday. To cut the cake, she makes 4 diameter cuts. How many pieces of cake does Jo cut?

_____

3. A 100-yard football field has markers drawn every ten yards, and at both ends. How many markers are drawn on the field? Complete the picture to prove your answer.

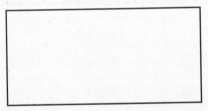

_____

4. Manchu makes some 1-inch cube blocks as a present for his little sister. He finds a box that is 2 inches tall, 4 inches wide, and 12 inches long. Will all 100 blocks fit in the box?

_____

5. James is playing with a flashlight. At what angle does he hold the light to see a perfect circle?

_____

Name _____ Date _____

 Write three other ways that you could read or write each fraction.

1. $\frac{1}{2}$ _____   2. $\frac{1}{8}$ _____   3. $\frac{3}{4}$ _____

_____   _____   _____

_____   _____   _____

 Write a fraction for the shaded part.

4.   5.   6.   7.

_____   _____   _____   _____

 Write the fraction.

8.

What part is shaded? _____

9.

What part is swimming? _____

10.

What part is on the log? _____

11.

What part is gray? _____

Real World Connection

Solve.

12. Jeana cut a watermelon into 8 equal pieces. She ate 3 pieces. What fraction of the watermelon was not eaten?

Name _____   Date _____

· · · · · · · · · JUST ANOTHER NAME · · · · · · · · ·

 Complete these equivalent fractions.

1. $\frac{1}{3} = \dfrac{\boxed{}}{6}$

2. $\frac{1}{2} = \dfrac{\boxed{}}{4}$

3. $\frac{3}{4} = \dfrac{\boxed{}}{8}$

4. $\frac{3}{9} = \dfrac{\boxed{}}{3}$

5. $\frac{6}{9} = \dfrac{\boxed{}}{3}$

6. $\frac{3}{6} = \dfrac{\boxed{}}{2}$

 Look at the first figure in each exercise. Then circle the figure that shows a fraction equivalent to the first figure.

7.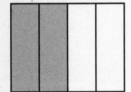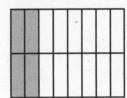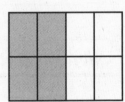

8.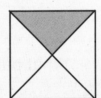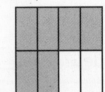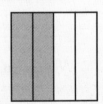

 Write two equivalent fractions for each.

9. $\frac{1}{4}$ ____ ____   10. $\frac{1}{5}$ ____ ____   11. $\frac{2}{3}$ ____ ____   12. $\frac{3}{8}$ ____ ____

Real World Connection

Solve.

13. Len uses $\frac{1}{4}$ of a dozen eggs to make pancakes. How many eggs does he use?

_____

Fractions: Equivalent Fractions

Math 4, SV 8048-0

Name _____   Date _____

Complete.

1. $\dfrac{3}{9} = \dfrac{\square}{3}$

2. $\dfrac{3}{12} = \dfrac{\square}{4}$

3. $\dfrac{8}{10} = \dfrac{\square}{5}$

4. $\dfrac{2}{12} = \dfrac{\square}{6}$

5. $\dfrac{10}{12} = \dfrac{10 \div 2}{12 \div 2} = \dfrac{\square}{\square}$

6. $\dfrac{3}{12} = \dfrac{3 \div 3}{12 \div 3} = \dfrac{\square}{\square}$

7. $\dfrac{5}{10} = \dfrac{5 \div \square}{10 \div \square} = \dfrac{\square}{2}$

8. $\dfrac{4}{20} = \dfrac{4 \div \square}{20 \div \square} = \dfrac{\square}{5}$

Write each fraction in simplest form.

9. $\dfrac{2}{14}$ _____

10. $\dfrac{3}{18}$ _____

11. $\dfrac{8}{28}$ _____

12. $\dfrac{4}{12}$ _____

Real World Connection

Solve.

13. It takes Josie 40 minutes to draw a picture. In simplest form, what part of an hour is 40 minutes?

_____

Name _____ Date _____

 Write the fraction for each figure. Then compare using <, >, or =.

1.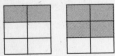

2.

_____   _____

Compare each pair of fractions using <, >, or =.

3. $\frac{1}{4}$ ◯ $\frac{2}{4}$ 4. $\frac{1}{2}$ ◯ $\frac{1}{4}$ 5. $\frac{4}{10}$ ◯ $\frac{9}{10}$

6. $\frac{4}{5}$ ◯ $\frac{3}{5}$ 7. $\frac{2}{6}$ ◯ $\frac{2}{3}$ 8. $\frac{2}{4}$ ◯ $\frac{2}{6}$

Compare. Write <, >, or =.

9. $\frac{1}{2}$ of 4 ◯ $\frac{1}{3}$ of 6   10. $\frac{1}{3}$ of 12 ◯ $\frac{1}{2}$ of 10

11. $\frac{5}{7}$ of 7 ◯ $\frac{1}{3}$ of 6   12. $\frac{1}{4}$ of 8 ◯ $\frac{1}{2}$ of 6

Use equivalent fractions to help you place each set in order from least to greatest.

13. $\frac{6}{10}, \frac{4}{10}, \frac{9}{10}$ _____   14. $\frac{1}{2}, \frac{5}{6}, \frac{1}{6}, \frac{2}{3}$ _____

Real World Connection

Solve.

15. Ming Lei used $\frac{2}{3}$ cup of raisins in her raisin bread. Elizabeth used $\frac{5}{8}$ cup of raisins in her raisin bread. Which girl used more raisins?

_____

Name _____   Date _____

 Write a mixed number for each picture.

1.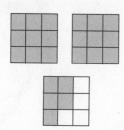

2.

_____   _____

3.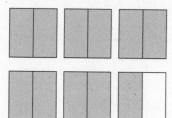

4.

_____   _____

 Write each fraction as a mixed number.

5. $\frac{11}{2}$ _____   6. $\frac{15}{7}$ _____   7. $\frac{14}{9}$ _____   8. $\frac{13}{4}$ _____

9. $\frac{10}{3}$ _____   10. $\frac{7}{2}$ _____   11. $\frac{11}{5}$ _____   12. $\frac{13}{3}$ _____

Real World Connection

Solve.

13. Shelly has $\frac{11}{2}$ pieces of apples to share with her friends. How many apples does she have? Write the number as a mixed number.

_____

········ **TALKING ABOUT FRACTIONS** ········

Find the sum. You may write the sum in simplest form.

1.  + =

$\frac{1}{3}$ + $\frac{1}{3}$ = ⬚/⬚

2.

$1\frac{1}{8}$ + $1\frac{5}{8}$ = ⬚/⬚

3. $\frac{1}{8} + \frac{4}{8} = \dfrac{\boxed{}}{8}$

4. $\frac{3}{10} + \frac{6}{10} = \dfrac{\boxed{}}{10}$

5. $2\frac{1}{6} + 1\frac{4}{6} = \underline{}\dfrac{\boxed{}}{6}$

6. $2\frac{1}{3}$
$+ 1\frac{1}{3}$

7. $1\frac{2}{4}$
$+ 3\frac{1}{4}$

8. $2\frac{4}{8}$
$+ 2\frac{3}{8}$

9. $1\frac{3}{10}$
$+ 3\frac{4}{10}$

10. $1\frac{3}{5}$
$+ 4\frac{1}{5}$

11. $\frac{1}{10}$
$+ \frac{7}{10}$

12. $2\frac{2}{7}$
$+ \frac{3}{7}$

13. $2\frac{1}{5}$
$+ 2\frac{3}{5}$

Real World Connection

Write the number sentence and solve.

14. Jailea talked $\frac{3}{12}$ of an hour to Diane and $\frac{4}{12}$ of an hour to Kim. What fraction of an hour did Jailea talk on the phone?

_____

Fractions: Adding Fractions and Mixed Numbers

Math 4, SV 8048-0

Name _____   Date _____

A BIKING DIFFERENCE

Find the difference. You may write the difference in simplest form.

1.

$\frac{8}{9} - \frac{2}{9} =$ _____

2.

$\frac{3}{4} - \frac{2}{4} =$ _____

3.

$5\frac{5}{8} - 2\frac{3}{8} =$ _____

4. $\frac{3}{4} - \frac{2}{4} = \dfrac{\boxed{}}{4}$

5. $\frac{3}{3} - \frac{2}{3} = \dfrac{\boxed{}}{3}$

6. $\frac{5}{10} - \frac{4}{10} = \dfrac{\boxed{}}{10}$

7. $\begin{array}{r}\frac{7}{7}\\[-2pt]-\frac{2}{7}\\\hline\end{array}$

8. $\begin{array}{r}\frac{10}{11}\\[-2pt]-\frac{4}{11}\\\hline\end{array}$

9. $\begin{array}{r}\frac{7}{9}\\[-2pt]-\frac{4}{9}\\\hline\end{array}$

10. $\begin{array}{r}\frac{5}{5}\\[-2pt]-\frac{3}{5}\\\hline\end{array}$

11. $\begin{array}{r}3\frac{5}{10}\\[-2pt]-1\frac{3}{10}\\\hline\end{array}$

12. $\begin{array}{r}7\frac{5}{6}\\[-2pt]-1\frac{4}{6}\\\hline\end{array}$

13. $\begin{array}{r}8\frac{3}{4}\\[-2pt]-2\frac{1}{4}\\\hline\end{array}$

14. $\begin{array}{r}2\frac{2}{4}\\[-2pt]-2\frac{1}{4}\\\hline\end{array}$

Real World Connection

Write the number sentence and solve.

15. The Cherry Bike Trail is $1\frac{6}{8}$ miles long. The Elm Bike Trail is $\frac{5}{8}$ miles long. How much longer is the Cherry Bike Trail than the Elm Bike Trail?

_____

········ PROBLEM SOLVING IN COLOR ·······

Choose the strategy and solve.

1. Awan makes a math game with 12 equal sections. Two sections are red, 4 sections are yellow, 4 sections are blue, and 2 sections are green. What two colors together cover more than $\frac{1}{2}$ of the spinner? Draw a model to solve.

_____

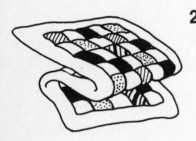

2. A quilt is made from panels of fabric. One third of the panels are made from plaid fabric, and one fourth of the panels are made from a flower print fabric. About how much of the quilt is plaid or a flower print?

_____

3. In a carton of zinnias, $\frac{3}{4}$ of them are red. How many are white?

_____

4. The pet store has 3 white kittens, 2 gray kittens, and 5 striped kittens. What fraction of gray kittens does the pet store have?

_____

5. Janna has $4\frac{2}{3}$ yards of blue fabric. She uses $1\frac{1}{3}$ yards to make a flag. How much fabric does Janna have left?

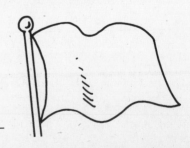

_____

• • • • • • • • POINTS ABOUT DECIMALS • • • • • • • •

 Make a model for each decimal. Then write as a fraction or mixed number and a decimal.

1. sixteen hundredths

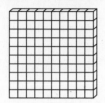

_____

2. five tenths

_____

3. seventy-five hundredths

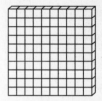

_____

4. one and forty-two hundredths

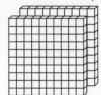

_____

5. one and three tenths

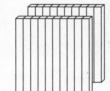

_____

6. one and seven hundredths

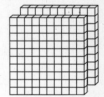

_____

Write the decimal.

7. $12\frac{3}{10}$ _____

8. $18\frac{70}{100}$ _____

9. $\frac{2}{100}$ _____

10. $6\frac{9}{10}$ _____

11. sixteen and two tenths _____

12. eight and six tenths _____

13. ten and ninety-nine hundredths _____

Real World Connection

Solve.

14. A decimal number has a 2 in the tens place, a 6 in the ones place, and a 7 in the hundredths place. Write the number.

_____

·········· MADE TO ORDER ··············

| Compare. Write <, >, or =. |

1.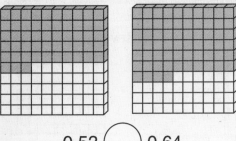

0.53 ◯ 0.64

2.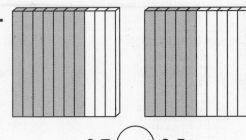

0.7 ◯ 0.5

3.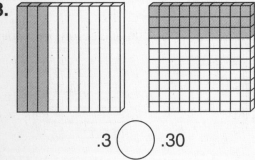

.3 ◯ .30

4.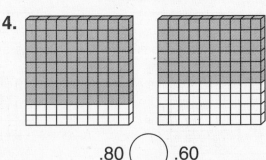

.80 ◯ .60

5. 0.8 ◯ 0.2   **6.** 2.26 ◯ 2.29   **7.** 32.54 ◯ 32.41

8. 0.18 ◯ 0.25   **9.** 96.30 ◯ 96.3   **10.** 27.18 ◯ 27.81

11. 3.07 ◯ 2.76   **12.** 16.9 ◯ 17   **13.** 31.6 ◯ 31.60

| Order the decimals from greatest to least. |

14. 3.5, 0.46, 5.8, 5.62   **15.** 52.43, 51.75, 51.7, 52.41

_____   _____

Real World Connection

Solve.

16. Pablo orders a hot dog that costs $1.50 and a
drink that costs $1.05. Which costs more?

_____

Name _____   Date _____

•••••• LOOK FOR "SUM" DIFFERENCE ••••••

Show each problem on the place-value chart. Solve.

1. 4.6 + 3.84 + 15.07 = _____

Tens	Ones	Tenths	Hundredths
___	___	___	___

2. 36.8 + 4.06 + 14.75 = _____

Tens	Ones	Tenths	Hundredths
___	___	___	___

3. 9.1 – 3.7 = ___

Ones	Tenths
___	___

4. 4.2 – 1.8 = ___

Ones	Tenths
___	___

5. 18.62 – 12.8 = _____

Tens	Ones	Tenths	Hundredths
___	___	___	___

Find the sum or difference.

6.   0.74
       + 0.08

7.   19.6
       + 4.7

8.   23.82
       + 18.56

9.   2.95
         14.86
       + 9.09

10.   7.8
        – 2.5

11.   5.63
        – 2.32

12.   42.06
        – 3.95

13.   72.45
        – 34.68

Real World Connection

Solve.

14. A package of turkey slices sells for $4.68 each or 2 packages for $9.04. Which is the better buy?

_____

Decimals: Adding and Subtracting Decimals

Math 4, SV 8048-0

FOURTH GRADE MATH

Answer Key

p. 5 1. 24 **2.** 54 **3.** 5 **4.** 6.95 **5.** 4,000 **6.** 27 **7.** 201
8. 6/8 or 3/4 **9.** 5,713 **10.** 2,072 **11.** 13,261 **12.** $11.77
13. 7,144 **14.** 83 r 4 **15.** 4 5/7 **16.** 40.92 **17.** 7,812
18. 2 3/9 or 2 1/3 **19.** 0 **20.** 162 **21.** 4 r 1 **22.** 68
23. 1,315 **24.** 588 **25.** 12 **26.** 3/10

p. 6 1. about $120 **2.** 3/3, 60 minutes **3.** 190 kilometers
4. 18 offices **5.** no **6.** 3/4 **7.** $2.64
8. 7 hours 45 minutes

p. 7 1. 3, 0, 300 **2.** 0, 4, 4 **3.** 8, 0, 80 **4.** 4, 0, 400 **5.** 60
6. 40 **7.** 9 **8.** 80 **9.** 70 **10.** 320 **11.** 3 thousands
8 hundreds; 38 hundreds; 380 tens; 3,800 ones
12. 1 thousand 4 hundreds; 14 hundreds; 140 tens;
1,400 ones **13.** 4 thousands 5 hundreds; 45 hundreds;
450 tens; 4,500 ones **14.** 3,700 gallons

p. 8 1. 10,607; ten thousand, six hundred seven
2. 90,500; 90,000 + 500 **3.** 30,000 + 4,000 + 60 + 9;
thirty-four thousand, sixty-nine **4.** three hundred seven
thousand, eight hundred sixty-four; 307,864
5. 400,000 + 600 + 70 + 3; 400,673 **6.** 20,000 + 400 +
80 + 3; twenty thousand, four hundred eighty-three
7. 400; 4 hundreds **8.** 40,000; 4 ten thousands **9.** 40;
4 tens **10.** 30,000; 3 ten thousands **11.** 0; 0 tens
12. 8,000; 8 thousands **13.** 289,300; 200,000 +
80,000 + 9,000 + 300

p. 9 1. thousands **2.** millions **3.** ones **4.** 68,016,018
5. 640,540,086 **6.** 21,876,905 **7.** 900,632,400
8. 13,579,410 **9.** 835,270,100 **10.** 37,850,298
11. 977,506,460 **12.** false **13.** true **14.** false **15.** true
16. 690,000,000 miles

p. 10 1. > **2.** < **3.** > **4.** < **5.** > **6.** < **7.** 52 < 56 **8.** 67 <
76 **9.** 1,239 < 1,339 **10.** 84 > 48 **11.** 2,094 > 2,049
12. 26,847 > 26,784 **13.** 763; 785; 812 **14.** 136; 149; 175
15. 929; 959; 990; 995 **16.** 4,364; 4,390; 4,618
17. 17,604; 17,640; 17,642; 17,697 **18.** Mesa Verde
National Park

p. 11 1. 50 **2.** $3.80 **3.** 70 **4.** $1.50 **5.** 90 **6.** $1.30
7. 560 **8.** 230 **9.** 910 **10.** 500 **11.** 200 **12.** $8.00
13. 200 **14.** $3.00 **15.** 900 **16.** 7,000 **17.** 2,000
18. 3,000 **19.** 1,000 **20.** 4,000 **21.** 8,000
22. least-375 cattle; greatest-384 cattle

p. 12 1. 3,915 miles **2.** 20,000 + 3,000 + 500 + 70 + 2
3. 2,348 > 2,315 **4.** 924 meters **5.** 4,200 miles

p. 13 1. 8, 10, 11 **2.** 6, 4, 2, 0 **3.** 3, 6, 7, 9 **4.** 17, 16, 15,
11 **5.** 6, 7, 8, 9 **6.** 5 **7.** 11 **8.** 7 **9.** 13 **10.** 8 **11.** 6
12. 7 + 8 = 15 computers

p. 14 1. 12; (3 + 5) + 4 = 12 **2.** 17; 2 + (7 + 8) = 17
3. 13; (4 + 1) + 8 = 13 **4.** 15; 4 + (5 + 6) = 15 **5.** 18;
(9 + 2) + 7 = 18 **6.** 14; 7 + (3 + 4) = 14 **7.** 12 **8.** 16
9. 16 **10.** 17 **11.** 14 **12.** 13 **13.** 14 **14.** 16 **15.** 18
16. 13 **17.** 16 **18.** 16 **19.** 11 **20.** 18 **21.** 13
22. 4 + 3 + 5 = 12 books

p. 15 1. $7.00 **2.** 700 **3.** $8.00 **4.** 700 **5.** $8.00 **6.** 600
7. 1,000 **8.** 7,000 **9.** $11.00 **10.** 900 **11.** $12 .00
12. 900 **13.** 8,000 **14.** $26.00 **15.** 4,000 **16.** 5,000
17. 55 + 86 = about 150 newspapers

p. 16 1. 59 **2.** 81 **3.** 65 **4.** 96 **5.** 150 **6.** 146 **7.** 128
8. 54 **9.** 78 **10.** 174 **11.** 60 **12.** 175 **13.** 140 **14.** 54
15. 98 **16.** 129 **17.** 163 **18.** 135 **19.** 135 **20.** 133
21. 116 **22.** 125 **23.** 65 + 78 = 143 seconds or
2 minutes 23 seconds

p. 17 1. 584 **2.** 935 **3.** 1,281 **4.** 1,259 **5.** 847 **6.** 1,125
7. $6.11 **8.** $3.84 **9.** $14.55 **10.** $11.77 **11.** 902
12. 1,366 **13.** 3,930 **14.** 10,305 **15.** 757 **16.** $11.20
17. $57.58 **18.** $7.90 **19.** $3.89 + $1.55 + $2.19 = $7.63

p. 18 1. 600 **2.** 400 **3.** 400 **4.** 300 **5.** 300 **6.** 3,000
7. 4,000 **8.** 2,000 **9.** $10.00 **10.** $20.00 **11.** 200
12. 500 **13.** $60.00 **14.** 4,000 **15.** 137 **16.** 1,570
17. more than 200 reptiles

p. 19 1. 54 **2.** 37 **3.** 11 **4.** 17 **5.** 4 **6.** 31 **7.** 51 **8.** 49
9. 39 **10.** 10 **11.** 42 **12.** 35 **13.** 2 **14.** 24 **15.** 45 **16.** 19
17. 8 **18.** 18 **19.** 26 **20.** 8 **21.** 56 **22.** 25 **23.** 13 **24.** 19
25. 51 **26.** 54 − 8 = 46 shovels

p. 20 1. 225 **2.** 495 **3.** 604 **4.** $6.80 **5.** $4.08 **6.** $5.68
7. 3,186 **8.** 3,928 **9.** 3,864 **10.** 754 **11.** 5,369
12. 3,159 **13.** 549 **14.** 824 **15.** $0.76 **16.** $2.94
17. 1,315 **18.** 1,081 **19.** 5,256 − 4,937 = 319 people

p. 21 1. 57 **2.** 13 **3.** 114 **4.** 48 **5.** 1,280 **6.** $6.87
7. 346 **8.** 9,100 **9.** 426 **10.** $18.69 **11.** 12,206
12. 8,052 **13.** 62,168 **14.** 401 **15.** 58 **16.** 117 **17.** $7.93
18. 591 **19.** 900 **20.** 4,481 **21.** 398 − 309 = 89 muffins

p. 22 1. $17 **2.** 6,038 pieces of clothing
3. about 100 more people **4.** 86 jackets **5.** $5.62

p. 23 1. 3 x 5 = 15 **2.** 4 x 6 = 24 **3.** 12 ÷ 4 = 3 or 12 ÷ 3
= 4 **4.** 20 ÷ 5 = 4 or 20 ÷ 4 = 5 **5.** 18 ÷ 6 = 3 or 18 ÷ 3 =
6 **6.** 6 x 8 = 48, 48 ÷ 6 = 8, 48 ÷ 8 = 6 **7.** 32 ÷ 8 = 4, 8 x
4 = 32, 4 x 8 = 32 **8.** 7 x 5 = 35, 35 ÷ 7 = 5, 35 ÷ 5 = 7
9. 9 x 3 = 27 minutes, 3 x 9 = 27, 27 ÷ 9 = 3, 27 ÷ 3 = 9

p. 24 1. 12; Students draw 2 groups of 6. **2.** 24;
Students draw 3 groups of 8. **3.** 2 **4.** 8 **5.** 3 **6.** 16
7. 18 **8.** 24 **9.** 18 **10.** 10 **11.** 12 **12.** 27 **13.** 14 **14.** 4
15. 12 **16.** 6 **17.** 15 **18.** 6 **19.** 21 **20.** 9 **21.** 24 **22.** 15
23. 12 **24.** 8 **25.** 21 **26.** 3 **27.** 2 x 8 = 16 students,
8 x 2 = 16, 16 ÷ 2 = 8, 16 ÷ 8 = 2

p. 25 1. 20; Students draw 4 groups of 5. **2.** 45;
Students draw 5 groups of 9. **3.** 15 **4.** 25 **5.** 4 **6.** 10
7. 24 **8.** 30 **9.** 12 **10.** 35 **11.** 32 **12.** 16 **13.** 20 **14.** 28
15. 45 **16.** 8 **17.** 5 **18.** 20 **19.** 40 **20.** 36 **21.** 40 **22.** 15
23. 35 **24.** 20 **25.** 28 **26.** 16 **27.** 7 x 4 = 28 boys,
4 x 7 = 28, 28 ÷ 4 = 7, 28 ÷ 7 = 4

p. 26 1. b **2.** d **3.** c **4.** d **5.** a **6.** a **7.** 35 **8.** 36 **9.** 18
10. 0 **11.** 0 **12.** 4 **13.** 24 **14.** 18 **15.** 0 **16.** < **17.** >
18. = **19.** > **20.** = **21.** < **22.** 4 x 0 = 0 paper clips

p. 27 42; Students draw 6 groups of 7. **2.** 28; Students
draw 7 groups of 4. **3.** 42 **4.** 6 **5.** 0 **6.** 42 **7.** 14 **8.** 28
9. 18 **10.** 49 **11.** 36 **12.** 30 **13.** 0 **14.** 7 **15.** 48 **16.** 56
17. 54 **18.** 36 **19.** 21 **20.** 54 **21.** 7 x 4 = 28 strings

p. 28 1. 27; Students draw 3 groups of 9. **2.** 64;
Students draw 8 groups of 8. **3.** 72 **4.** 24 **5.** 9 **6.** 56
7. 18 **8.** 8 **9.** 63 **10.** 32 **11.** 0 **12.** 64 **13.** 54 **14.** 16
15. 45 **16.** 48 **17.** 81 **18.** 27 **19.** 36 **20.** 40
21. 8 x 6 = 48 slices

p. 29 1. 24, 32, 40, 48, 56, 64, 72 **2.** 21, 28, 35, 42, 49,
56, 63 **3.** 24 **4.** 54 **5.** 32 **6.** 18 **7.** 56 **8.** 20 **9.** 0
10. 16 **11.** 72 **12.** 24 **13.** 35 **14.** 81 **15.** 28 **16.** 30
17. 63 **18.** 16 **19.** 0 **20.** 42 **21.** 64 **22.** 21 **23.** 48
24. 6 **25.** 36 **26.** 0 **27.** 5 x 6 = 30 eggs

Math 4, SV 8048-0

p. 30 1. 6; 60; 600; 6,000 **2.** 12; 120; 1,200; 12,000
3. 4; 280; 400; 28,000 For **4.–7.** check students' work.
4. 717 **5.** 184 **6.** 610 **7.** 152 **8.** $18 x 4 = $72

p. 31 1. 248 **2.** 201 **3.** 246 **4.** 234 **5.** 837 **6.** 208 **7.** 96
8. 170 **9.** 186 **10.** 414 **11.** 94 **12.** 180 **13.** 180 **14.** 117
15. 216 **16.** 162 **17.** 504 **18.** 225 **19.** 132 **20.** 168
21. 168 **22.** 4 x 26 = 104 bags

p. 32 1. 574 **2.** 342 **3.** 951 **4.** 875 **5.** 744 **6.** 728
7. 770 **8.** 957 **9.** 680 **10.** 984 **11.** 1,968 **12.** 1,892
13. 1,953 **14.** 915 **15.** 4,192 **16.** 7,144 **17.** 13,095
18. 29,032 **19.** 954 **20.** 1,602 **21.** 25,368 **22.** 27,798
23. 1,086 x 3 = 3,258 newspapers

p. 33 1. $7.00 x 3 = $21.00, $19.14 **2.** $0.80 x 9 = $7.20,
$6.48 **3.** $5.00 x 6 = $30.00, $27.12 **4.** $50.00 x 3 =
$150.00, $128.55 **5.** $20.00 x 4 = $80.00, $63.04
6. $6.00 x 4 = $24.00, $21.16 **7.** $0.90 x 5 = $4.50, $4.10
8. $50.00 x 6 = $300.00, $280.26 **9.** $26.46
10. $1.41 **11.** $11.60 **12.** $2.97 **13.** $8.05 **14.** $14.08
15. 6 x $9.40 = $56.40

p. 34 1. 10 x 60 = 600 **2.** 40 x 20 = 800 **3.** 60 x 80 =
4,800 **4.** 30 x 10 = 300 **5.** 10 x 60 = 600 **6.** 40 x 30 =
1,200 **7.** 60 x 90 = 5,400 **8.** 30 x 20 = 600 **9.** $100
10. $540 **11.** $50 **12.** $68.00 **13.** $154.00 **14.** $77.00
15. 20 x 60 = 1,200 houses

p. 35 1. 1,824 **2.** 3,456 **3.** 1,428 **4.** 2,790 **5.** 1,896
6. 3,648 **7.** 897 **8.** 6,750 **9.** 1,827 **10.** 2,352 **11.** 2,112
12. 1,888 **13.** 4,224 **14.** 2,014 **15.** 3,120 **16.** 2,394
17. 1,118 **18.** 3,128 **19.** 36 x 21 = 756 miles

p. 36 1. 4,140 **2.** 23,256 **3.** 8,692 **4.** 24,928
5. 58,473 **6.** 9,396 **7.** 49,742 **8.** $1,197.98 **9.** $7,504.44
10. 900,720 **11.** 45,212 **12.** 15,996 **13.** 34,328
14. 30,720 **15.** 121,512 **16.** 32,220
17. 42 x 250 = 10,500 bulbs

p. 37 1. 56 **2.** 0 **3.** 135 **4.** $8.22 **5.** 3,336 **6.** 25,808
7. 2,240 **8.** 768 **9.** 4,402 **10.** 7,812 **11.** 9 **12.** 138
13. 1,200 **14.** 1,600 **15.** 18,179 **16.** 64,875
17. 37 x 14 = 518 acorns

p. 38 1. no **2.** 2,184 hours **3.** 648 miles **4.** $20,076
5. 105 trucks

p. 39 1. 3 x 4 = 12, 12 ÷ 3 = 4 or 12 ÷ 4 = 3 **2.** 3 x 6 =
18, 18 ÷ 6 = 3 or 18 ÷ 3 = 6 **3.** 6 x 8 = 48, 48 ÷ 6 = 8, 48
÷ 8 = 6 **4.** 56 ÷ 8 = 7, 8 x 7 = 56, 7 x 8 = 56 **5.** 7 x 6 =
42, 42 ÷ 6 = 7, 42 ÷ 7 = 6 **6.** 9, 4 x 9 = 36 or 9 x 4 = 36
7. 7, 35 ÷ 5 = 7 or 35 ÷ 7 = 5 **8.** 8, 72 ÷ 9 = 8 or 72 ÷ 8
= 9 **9.** 14 ÷ 2 = 7 bags

p. 40 1. 3; Students draw 3 groups of 3. **2.** 6; Students
draw 2 groups of 6. **3.** 9 **4.** 1 **5.** 6 **6.** 2 **7.** 4 **8.** 7 **9.** 8
10. 2 **11.** 9 **12.** 8 **13.** 2 **14.** 5 **15.** 8 **16.** 3 **17.** 5 **18.** 6
19. 4 **20.** 1 **21.** 7 **22.** 5 **23.** 9 **24.** 18 ÷ 2 = 9 shells

p. 41 1. 5; Students draw 4 groups of 5. **2.** 5; Students
draw 5 groups of 5. **3.** 8 **4.** 7 **5.** 3 **6.** 8 **7.** 7 **8.** 4 **9.** 5
10. 5 **11.** 3 **12.** 6 **13.** 9 **14.** 2 **15.** 1 **16.** 9 **17.** 6 **18.** 5
19. 7 **20.** 4 **21.** 3 **22.** 4 **23.** 1 **24.** 24 ÷ 4 = 6 days

p. 42 1. 0 **2.** 1 **3.** 1 **4.** 0 **5.** 18 **6.** 1 **7.** 64 **8.** 7 **9.** 0
10. 1 **11.** 17 **12.** 0 **13.** 1 **14.** 1 **15.** 0 **16.** 1 **17.** 3 **18.** 1
19. 1 **20.** 0 **21.** 1 **22.** 24 **23.** 8 **24.** 0 **25.** 1 **26.** 0
27. 10 **28.** 1 **29.** 7 ÷ 7 = 1 pin

p. 43 1. 5; Students draw 7 groups of 5 **2.** 6; Students
draw 6 groups of 6. **3.** 2 **4.** 7 **5.** 3 **6.** 9 **7.** 5 **8.** 9 **9.** 4
10. 4 **11.** 2 **12.** 7 **13.** 1 **14.** 8 **15.** 3 **16.** 1 **17.** 6 **18.** 8
19. 7 **20.** 5 **21.** 2 **22.** 0 **23.** 6 **24.** 24 ÷ 6 = 4 trips

p. 44 1. 4; Students draw 9 groups of 4. **2.** 5; Students
draw 8 groups of 5. **3.** 7 **4.** 2 **5.** 3 **6.** 7 **7.** 4 **8.** 1 **9.** 6
10. 8 **11.** 6 **12.** 8 **13.** 1 **14.** 2 **15.** 9 **16.** 3 **17.** 3 **18.** 7
19. 2 **20.** 4 **21.** 5 **22.** 0 **23.** 9 **24.** 56 ÷ 8 = 7 roses

p. 45 1. 7 **2.** 0 **3.** 4 **4.** 9 **5.** 5 **6.** 4 **7.** 9 **8.** 7 **9.** 4
10. 8 **11.** 4 **12.** 5 **13.** 7 **14.** 3 **15.** 8 **16.** 9 **17.** 8 **18.** 1
19. 7 **20.** 8 **21.** 7 **22.** 8 **23.** 4 **24.** 5 **25.** 72 ÷ 9 =
8 pieces of paper

p. 46 1. 3 **2.** 4 **3.** 1 **4.** 3 **5.** 4, 40, 400 **6.** 3, 30, 300
7. 8, 80, 800 **8.** 7, 70, 700, 7,000 **9.** 8, 80, 800, 8,000
10. 9, 90, 900, 9,000 **11.** 5, 50, 500, 5,000
12. 1,200 ÷ 6 = 200 books

p. 47 1. 15 **2.** 24 **3.** 23 **4.** 13 **5.** 21 **6.** 18 **7.** 15 **8.** 13
9. 11 **10.** 27 **11.** 24 **12.** 15 **13.** 14 **14.** 16 **15.** 12
16. 14 **17.** 64 ÷ 4 = 16 students

p. 48 1. x in ones **2.** x in tens **3.** x in ones **4.** x in tens
For **5.–13.** check students' work. **5.** 17 **6.** 13 r 3 **7.** 13 r 4
8. 24 **9.** 21 r 3 **10.** 13 **11.** 29 r 2 **12.** 11 r 5
13. 7 r 2 **14.** 52 ÷ 3 = 17 r 1, 17 sandwiches with
1 slice remaining

p. 49 1. b **2.** c **3.** a **4.** 50 **5.** 60 **6.** 40 **7.** 30 **8.** 20
9. 70 **10.** 80 **11.** 20 **12.** 80 **13.** 80 **14.** 30 **15.** 60
16. 60 **17.** 70 **18.** 90 **19.** 70 **20.** 238 ÷ 3 = about
80 seats

p. 50 1. x in tens **2.** x in hundreds **3.** x in hundreds
4. x in hundreds For **5.–13.**, check students' work.
5. 84 r 2 **6.** 65 **7.** 122 r 5 **8.** 83 r 4 **9.** 55 r 2
10. 81 r 1 **11.** 280 r 1 **12.** 143 r 1 **13.** 90
14. 875 ÷ 9 = 97 r 2 compact discs

p. 51 1. x in the tens **2.** x in the tens **3.** x in the
hundreds **4.** x in the hundreds **5.** 100, 103 r 1
6. 200, 202 r 1 **7.** 100, 107 r 3 **8.** 200, 205 r 2 **9.** 300,
306 **10.** 100, 106 r 4 **11.** 100 r 2 **12.** 100 r 1
13. 200 r 3 **14.** 812 ÷ 4 = 203 cars

p. 52 For **1.–10.** check students' work. **1.** $0.93 **2.** $1.70
3. $2.04 **4.** $0.87 **5.** $0.79 **6.** $1.20 **7.** $1.30 **8.** $4.07
9. $0.68 **10.** $1.15 **11.** $9.72 ÷ 2 = $4.86

p. 53 1. 6, 6, 60 **2.** 9, 9, 90 **3.** 5, 5, 50 **4.** 8, 8, 8 **5.** 4,
12 ÷ 3= 4 **6.** 8, 16 ÷ 2 = 8 **7.** 7, 28 ÷ 4 = 7 **8.** 6, 30 ÷ 5
= 6 **9.** 160 ÷ 40 = 4 days

p. 54 1. x in the ones **2.** x in the ones **3.** x in the ones
4. x in the ones For **5.–13.**, check students' work.
5. 2 r 8 **6.** 4 r 8 **7.** 5 r 31 **8.** 5 r 18 **9.** 7 r 15
10. 6 r 20 **11.** 9 r 25 **12.** 5 r 11 **13.** 5 r 27
14. 190 ÷ 20 = 9 r 10, 9 rows and 10 extra people

p. 55 1. 4 r 1 **2.** 4 r 2 **3.** 3 r 1 **4.** 3 r 7 **5.** 5 r 3 **6.** 4 r 1
7. 2 r 57 **8.** 5 **9.** 5 r 17 **10.** 4 r 8 **11.** 7 r 10 **12.** 5 r 20
13. 7 **14.** 6 r 9 **15.** 115 ÷ 23 = 5 rides

p. 56 1. x in the tens **2.** x in the tens **3.** x in the tens
4. x in the ones **5.** 2, 2 r 11 **6.** 4, 3 r 49 **7.** 4, 4 r 7
8. 28 r 9 **9.** 16 r 6 **10.** 12 r 16 **11.** 15 r 22 **12.** 36
13. 6 **14.** 23 **15.** 12 **16.** 204 ÷ 17 = 12 people

p. 57 1. 7 **2.** 6 r 4 **3.** 4 r 7 **4.** 2 **5.** 71 r 2 **6.** 20 **7.** 92
8. $0.79 **9.** 86 **10.** 7 r 17 **11.** 9 **12.** 13 **13.** 16
14. 2 r 8 **15.** 90 **16.** 6 **17.** 64 ÷ 4 = 16 days

p. 58 1. 100 students **2.** 10 photographs **3.** $53
4. 16 weeks **5.** no

p. 59 1. 7:15, seven-fifteen, 15 minutes past seven, a quarter past 7 **2.** 4:43, four forty-three, forty-three minutes past four, seventeen minutes to five **3.** 8:30, eight-thirty, thirty minutes past eight, a half past eight **4.** 3:45, three forty-five, forty-five minutes past three, fifteen minutes to four **5.** 6:04 **6.** 7:37 **7.** Jason prepared the bread dough.

p. 60 1. months **2.** minutes **3.** minutes **4.** second **5.** 15 minutes **6.** 8 hours **7.** 4:00 or 3:55

p. 61 1. 16 hours **2.** 65 minutes or 1 hour, 5 minutes **3.** 35 minutes **4.** 5 hours **5.** 7:45 A.M. **6.** 35 minutes

p. 62 1. May 6 **2.** May 14 **3.** May 17 **4.** Friday, May 25 **5.** Friday, May 18 **6.** Monday, May 14

p. 63 1. basketball **2.** 24 people **3.** 42 people **4.** Soccer-6, Tennis-4, Swimming-8, Basketball-15, Football-9 **5.** 74 more visitors **6.** Game 4 **7.** Game 5, Game 2, Game 3, Game 1, Game 4 **8.** Answers will vary.

p. 64 1. Wednesday **2.** Tuesday **3.** Wednesday-20, Friday-80, Monday-60 **4.** 80 more boxes **5.** 420 boxes **6.** Answers will vary.

p. 65 1. horizontal **2.** the number of students **3.** 10 students **4.** painting **5.** clay modeling **6.** Check students' bar graphs.

p. 66 1. Saturday **2.** Monday **3.** Wednesday-200, Friday-250, Monday-50 **4.** Check student's graphs.

p. 67 1. X **2.** R **3.** C **4.** P **5.** U **6.** L **7.** (8, 3) **8.** (0, 4) **9.** (8,10) **10.** (6, 6) **11.** (2, 8) **12.** (7, 9) **13.** THAT HITS THE SPOT **14.** Answers will vary.

p. 68 1. 7:57 A. M. **2.** Check students' work. **3.** Check students' graphs. **4.** 104 people **5.** $24

p. 69 For **1.–7.**, check students' measurements. **8.** Check students' rectangle measurements. **9.** No; 45 + 45 = 90 inches, which is less than the 96 inches Lee needs.

p. 70 1. inches **2.** feet **3.** yards **4.** feet **5.** 3 yd **6.** 16 ft **7.** 23 mi. **8.** 400 yd **9.** Mississippi **10.** 1,040 mi. **11.** Bruster; 246 + 84 = 330 miles, which is shorter than 206 + 192 = 398 miles going through Capital City.

p. 71 1. gallon **2.** cup **3.** gallon **4.** quart **5.** tablespoon **6.** cup or pint **7.** 2 tbsp **8.** 4 pt **9.** 10 gal **10.** cups **11.** cup or pint **12.** 2 pints

p. 72 1. ounce **2.** pound **3.** pound **4.** ton **5.** pound **6.** ounce or pound **7.** 1 lb **8.** 7 lb **9.** 5 oz **10.** 80 **11.** 26,000 **12.** 4 **13.** 3 pounds

p. 73 1. 2 cm **2.** 6 cm **3.** 1 dm **4.** centimeter or decimeter **5.** meter **6.** kilometer **7.** centimeter **8.** 5 dm **9.** 10 m **10.** 16 km **11.** 2 m **12.** 7 x 7 = 49 km

p. 74 1. liters **2.** milliliters **3.** liters **4.** milliliters **5.** 1 mL **6.** 500 mL **7.** 120 mL **8.** c **9.** b **10.** b **11.** the wide vase

p. 75 1. grams **2.** grams **3.** kilograms **4.** kilograms **5.** grams **6.** kilograms **7.** 1 g **8.** 1,750 kg **9.** 20 g **10.** 450 kg **11.** 725 grams

p. 76 1. yes **2.** 1 gallon **3.** 8 ounces **4.** 4 liters **5.** no

p. 77 1. solid **2.** plane **3.** plane **4.** solid **5.** rectangular prism **6.** cylinder **7.** cone **8.** pyramid **9.** cone **10.** sphere **11.** cube **12.** rectangular prism **13.** rectangle and triangle

p. 78 1. line segment **2.** ray **3.** point **4.** line For **5.–7.** check students' drawings. **8.** no **9.** yes **10.** no **11.** no **12.** Possible answers include ●→ LK, ●→ LD, ●→ LB, ●→ LM, ●→ LN **13.** ←→ NM, ←→ DB **14.** a star

p. 79 1. acute **2.** right **3.** obtuse **4.** acute **5.** right **6.** obtuse **7.** acute **8.** obtuse **9.** right **10.** 3 **11.** 2 **12.** 3 **13.** 1 **14.** acute

p. 80 1. Check students' drawings. **2.** 3 cm **3.** 6 cm **4.** point m **5.** Possible answers include radii MA, MT, MH **6.** AH **7.** diameter **8.** point S **9.** radius **10.** diameter **11.** right angles

p. 81 1. 2 cm x 3 cm x 4 cm = 24 cubic cm **2.** 5 cm x 3 cm x 5 cm = 75 cubic cm **3.** 4 cm x 5 cm x 8 cm = 160 cm **4.** 6 cm x 7 cm x 1 cm = 42 cubic cm **5.** 4 cm x 9 cm x 3 cm = 108 cubic cm **6.** 5 cm x 2 cm x 6 cm = 60 cm **7.** 64 cubic cm **8.** 30 cubic cm **9.** 24 cubic cm **10.** 3 cm **11.** 6 cm **12.** 1,053 cubic inches of water

p. 82 1. Possible answer: a cube and a pyramid **2.** 8 pieces **3.** 11 markers. **4.** no **5.** 90°

p. 83 1. one half, one out of two, one divided by two **2.** one eighth, one out of eight, one divided by eight **3.** three fourths, three out of four, three divided by four **4.** 2/5 **5.** 3/4 **6.** 1/2 **7.** 5/8 **8.** 1/8 **9.** 4/6 or 2/3 **10.** 3/5 **11.** 1/2 **12.** 5/8 of the watermelon

p. 84 1. 2 **2.** 2 **3.** 6 **4.** 1 **5.** 2 **6.** 1 **7.** Students circle figure showing 4/8. **8.** Students circle figure showing 6/8. For **9.–12.** answers will vary. **13.** 3 eggs

p. 85 1. 1 **2.** 1 **3.** 4 **4.** 1 **5.** 5/6 **6.** 1/4 **7.** 5/5, 1 **8.** 4/4, 1 **9.** 1/7 **10.** 1/6 **11.** 2/7 **12.** 1/3 **13.** 2/3 hour

p. 86 1. 1/3 < 4/5 **2.** 4/5 > 6/10 **3.** < **4.** > **5.** < **6.** > **7.** < **8.** > **9.** = **10.** < **11.** > **12.** < **13.** 4/10, 6/10, 9/10 **14.** 1/6, 1/2, 2/3, 5/6 **15.** Ming Lei

p. 87 1. 2 5/9 **2.** 1 3/8 **3.** 5 1/2 **4.** 1 7/9 **5.** 5 1/2 **6.** 2 1/7 **7.** 1 5/9 **8.** 3 1/4 **9.** 3 1/3 **10.** 3 1/2 **11.** 2 1/5 **12.** 4 1/3 **13.** 5 1/2 apples

p. 88 1. 2/3 **2.** 2 6/8 or 2 3/4 **3.** 5/8 **4.** 9/10 **5.** 3 5/6 **6.** 3 2/3 **7.** 4 3/4 **8.** 4 7/8 **9.** 4 7/10 **10.** 5 4/5 **11.** 8/10 or 4/5 **12.** 2 5/7 **13.** 4 4/5 **14.** 7/12 of an hour

p. 89 1. 6/9 or 2/3 **2.** 1/4 **3.** 3 2/8 or 3 1/4 **4.** 1 **5.** 1 **6.** 1 **7.** 5/7 **8.** 6/11 **9.** 3/9 or 1/3 **10.** 2/5 **11.** 2 2/10 or 2 1/5 **12.** 6 1/6 **13.** 6 2/4 or 6 1/2 **14.** 1/4 **15.** 1 6/8 - 5/8 = 1 1/8 miles more

p. 90 1. blue and yellow-Check students' drawings. **2.** about 1/2 of the quilt **3.** 1/4 white zinnias **4.** 2/10 or 1/5 gray kittens **5.** 3 1/3 yards fabric

p. 91 1. 16/100, .16 **2.** 5/10, .5 **3.** 75/100, .75 **4.** 1 42/100, 1.42 **5.** 1 3/10, 1.3 **6.** 1 7/100, 1.07 **7.** 12.3 **8.** 18.70 **9.** .02 **10.** 6.9 **11.** 16.2 **12.** 8.6 **13.** 10.99 **14.** 26.07

p. 92 1. < **2.** > **3.** = **4.** > **5.** > **6.** < **7.** > **8.** < **9.** = **10.** < **11.** > **12.** < **13.** = **14.** 5.8, 5.62, 3.5, 0.46 **15.** 52.43, 52.41, 51.75, 51.7 **16.** hot dog

p. 93 For **1.–5.** check students' work. **1.** 23.51 **2.** 55.61 **3.** 5.4 **4.** 2.4 **5.** 5.82 **6.** 0.82 **7.** 24.3 **8.** 42.38 **9.** 26.90 **10.** 5.3 **11.** 3.31 **12.** 38.11 **13.** 37.77 **14.** 2 packages for $9.04